NEW DIRECTIONS FOR EVALUATION
A Publication of the American Evaluation Association

Gary T. Henry, *Georgia State University*
COEDITOR-IN-CHIEF

Jennifer C. Greene, *Cornell University*
COEDITOR-IN-CHIEF

# Current and Emerging Ethical Challenges in Evaluation

Jody L. Fitzpatrick
*University of Colorado*

Michael Morris
*University of New Haven*

EDITORS

Number 82, Summer 1999

JOSSEY-BASS PUBLISHERS
San Francisco

CURRENT AND EMERGING ETHICAL CHALLENGES IN EVALUATION
*Jody L. Fitzpatrick, Michael Morris* (eds.)
New Directions for Evaluation, no. 82
*Jennifer C. Greene, Gary T. Henry,* Coeditors-in-Chief

Microfilm copies of issues and articles are available in 16mm and 35mm, as well as microfiche in 105mm, through University Microfilms Inc., 300 North Zeeb Road, Ann Arbor, Michigan 48106-1346.

*New Directions for Evaluation* is indexed in Contents Pages in Education, Higher Education Abstracts, and Sociological Abstracts.

ISSN 0197-6736        ISBN 0-7879-4902-7

NEW DIRECTIONS FOR EVALUATION is part of The Jossey-Bass Education Series and is published quarterly by Jossey-Bass Inc., Publishers, 350 Sansome Street, San Francisco, California 94104–1342.

SUBSCRIPTIONS cost $65.00 for individuals and $115.00 for institutions, agencies, and libraries. Prices subject to change.

EDITORIAL CORRESPONDENCE should be addressed to the Coeditors-in-Chief, Jennifer C. Greene, Department of Policy Analysis and Management, MVR Hall, Cornell University, Ithaca, NY 14853-4401, or Gary T. Henry, School of Policy Studies, Georgia State University, P.O. Box 4039, Atlanta, GA 30302-4039.

Cover design by Design Office.

www.josseybass.com

# EDITORIAL POLICY AND PROCEDURES

*New Directions for Evaluation,* a quarterly sourcebook, is an official publication of the American Evaluation Association. The journal publishes empirical, methodological, and theoretical works on all aspects of evaluation. A reflective approach to evaluation is an essential strand to be woven through every volume. The editors encourage volumes that have one of three foci: (1) craft volumes that present approaches, methods, or techniques that can be applied in evaluation practice, such as the use of templates, case studies, or survey research; (2) professional issue volumes that present issues of import for the field of evaluation, such as utilization of evaluation or locus of evaluation capacity; (3) societal issue volumes that draw out the implications of intellectual, social, or cultural developments for the field of evaluation, such as the women's movement, communitarianism, or multiculturalism. A wide range of substantive domains is appropriate for *New Directions for Evaluation;* however, the domains must be of interest to a large audience within the field of evaluation. We encourage a diversity of perspectives and experiences within each volume, as well as creative bridges between evaluation and other sectors of our collective lives.

The editors do not consider or publish unsolicited single manuscripts. Each issue of the journal is devoted to a single topic, with contributions solicited, organized, reviewed, and edited by a guest editor. Issues may take any of several forms, such as a series of related chapters, a debate, or a long article followed by brief critical commentaries. In all cases, the proposals must follow a specific format, which can be obtained from the editor-in-chief. These proposals are sent to members of the editorial board and to relevant substantive experts for peer review. The process may result in acceptance, a recommendation to revise and resubmit, or rejection. However, the editors are committed to working constructively with potential guest editors to help them develop acceptable proposals.

Jennifer C. Greene, Coeditor-in-Chief
Department of Policy Analysis and Management
MVR Hall
Cornell University
Ithaca, NY 14853-4401
e-mail: jcg8@cornell.edu

Gary T. Henry, Coeditor-in-Chief
School of Policy Studies
Georgia State University
P.O. Box 4039
Atlanta, GA 30302-4039
e-mail: gthenry@gsu.edu

# CONTENTS

# EDITORS' NOTES

In 1995 the American Evaluation Association (AEA) published its *Guiding Principles for Evaluators*. By virtue of being principles, these guidelines were general. (Indeed, Peter Rossi argued they were misleading in their ambiguity.) However, the principles, adopted as the ethical code by AEA, were designed to stimulate further dialogue, not solely about the principles themselves but also about what constitutes ethical behavior in the profession of evaluation. This volume is intended to serve that purpose. We hope that the issues raised here will also stimulate further discussion about the ethical challenges that evaluators face. It is only through discussion of particular cases and issues that we can move toward clarity and consensus about ethical behavior.

Program evaluation faces environmental changes today that will challenge our ethical practices. Devolution, or the delegation of more services to state and local governments, and the related issues of privatization are changing evaluation clients and our relationships with them, other stakeholders, and the general public. Removal of service delivery from the public sector, though holding the promise of improving efficiency and, perhaps, effectiveness, changes the role of government. What will the role of evaluation be in such settings? It may be more difficult for evaluators to address the public good or the interests of certain client groups when services are delivered through the private sector. Conversely, privatizing is designed to enable services to be delivered with greater flexibility. What should the evaluator do if government oversight, often via evaluation, becomes so onerous that flexibility cannot be attained?

Another environmental change is the increased attention being directed toward outcomes as exhibited through (1) the federal government's Government Performance and Results Act (GPRA), (2) the outcomes focus being promulgated by United Way (and thus affecting many nonprofit organizations funded by United Way), and (3) the standards focus in education. These shifts in emphasis were initiated as a result of frustration with many organizations' preoccupation with process rather than outcomes. Evaluators can applaud the movement toward articulating logic models and outcomes. However, as evaluators, we know that risks are entailed in measuring outcomes solely or prematurely. Programs need time to tinker with their model, adapting it to their particular clients' needs and organization's resources. Formative evaluation can be vital at these stages. Evaluators have found, in fact, that the results of formative evaluations are often more readily used than those from summative studies.

Though the outcomes initiatives promise that more summative decisions will result from the more useful outcome-oriented findings, we remain skeptical because of what we have learned about decision making. We long ago abandoned a strict Tylerian approach to objectives as the sole focus of evaluation. What actions should evaluators take when organizations are forced to evaluate outcomes too early? What actions should we take when evaluation monies, which could be used more fruitfully for formative needs assessment or process questions, are diverted to outcomes to meet external mandates? These new environments will present different, and challenging, ethical conflicts for evaluators. To confront these challenges and to serve society successfully, we must continue the dialogue, defining who we are and what we should be doing.

We have used, as a framework for this volume, the five roles developed by Newman and Brown in *Applied Ethics for Program Evaluation:* consultant/administrator, data collector/researcher, reporter, member of profession, and member of society. In each role, different ethical dilemmas and issues are encountered. As appropriate, we draw on particular AEA Guiding Principles and Standards, but these are not our sole focus. Instead, we consider selected ethical issues that evaluators encounter in each of these roles, and discuss conflicts that may arise and the means by which such conflicts might be avoided, reduced, or resolved. These "means" are not simple answers, but instead are approaches to assist individual evaluators in formulating their own ethical "solutions."

The issue begins with two chapters we have written that serve as a foundation for the volume. The first chapter, by Jody L. Fitzpatrick, reviews the history of ethical codes in evaluation and relates our progress and concerns to those of related disciplines and professions. Reviewing writings concerning professional ethics in general and the codes of other associations in particular, she makes recommendations concerning how we should progress as a profession in using ethical codes to encourage ethical behavior in evaluators. In the second chapter, Michael Morris describes what we have learned about ethical behavior among evaluators through empirical research. His review illustrates the lack of consensus in evaluation on what constitutes ethical behavior, but also provides some lessons on the "hot button" areas where we should be sensitive to ethical conflicts.

The remaining chapters address the roles articulated by Newman and Brown. In Chapter Three, Sandra Mathison discusses one of the first issues confronted by an evaluator as consultant/administrator, the dilemmas of context or community. She believes there are more similarities than differences in the dilemmas confronted by internal and external evaluators, but argues that important differences emerge in how they can resolve ethical dilemmas and, to a certain extent, what types of ethical dilemmas each can most successfully address. David Nee and Maria I. Mojica, in Chapter Four, also address the ethical roles of evaluators in their consultant/administrator role. They describe the ethical challenges evaluators will face in the new, more collaborative roles that foundations are seeking from evaluators. Nee and Mojica are managers of a foundation that has undertaken these endeavors; therefore, they provide an important user's perspective on ethical concerns in evaluation.

In Chapter Five Melvin M. Mark, Kristen M. Eyssell, and Bernadette Campbell examine ethical conflicts that evaluators face in their central role as data collectors/researchers. They argue that the quality of the research design that the evaluator selects is an important ethical issue and describe a cost-benefit approach to exploring the ethics of various designs. They also argue that evaluators have an ethical obligation to explore their data thoroughly, a contention that upsets the quantitative traditions regarding testing only *a priori* hypotheses.

Rosalie T. Torres and Hallie Preskill in Chapter Six examine ethical problems involved in the equally important role of the evaluator as reporter. As they note, the reporter role reflects the evaluator's ethical obligation for utility or, ideally, use. As many in evaluation have noted, use does not necessarily follow from a well-written report or an excellent methodology. Instead, use results from careful consideration of stakeholders throughout the evaluation. Participatory evaluation and empowerment evaluation have introduced new roles for stakeholders that can facilitate use in different ways. Torres and Preskill discuss the ethical concerns evaluators must consider in using stakeholder involvement to facilitate use or change.

Serving as a member of one's profession includes considering ways to educate and train evaluators, and other audiences, concerning evaluation ethics. Dianna L. Newman argues in Chapter Seven for the need of a core curriculum and takes a leap in that direction by discussing the content areas she believes must be addressed to enable those in our profession to behave ethically.

The final role in which an evaluator serves is that of a member of society. Two ethically related concerns are the controversial issue of evaluators' acting as advocates and the concerns evaluators face when working in a society (culture) that is different from their own. Lois-ellin Datta reviews, in Chapter Eight, the writings of prominent evaluation scholars regarding advocacy and finds more consensus than one might have expected. She argues that most writers in this area agree that evaluators should seek broad stakeholder involvement and few believe that evaluators should go much beyond that. The evaluator's obligation is to ensure that all voices are heard, an obligation that often involves advocating for the inclusion of stakeholders whose voices have been muted in the past. Michael Bamberger, with extensive experience conducting evaluations in developing countries, in Chapter Nine discusses two issues that can create ethical dilemmas when evaluators work in these settings: the extent to which evaluators should respect the customs and values of the host country, and the nature of stakeholder involvement. As always, examining issues in other countries can sensitize us to similar concerns in our own.

Jody L. Fitzpatrick
Michael Morris
Editors

JODY L. FITZPATRICK is associate professor of public administration at the University of Colorado. She maintains an active practice in evaluation and is interested in the ethical nuances of evaluator-client relations. She serves on the Board of the American Evaluation Association and is working on a book of case studies for the association.

MICHAEL MORRIS is professor of psychology and director of graduate field training in community psychology at the University of New Haven. He edits the column "Ethical Challenges" in the American Journal of Evaluation.

*The author argues that insufficient attention has been given to the study of ethical codes in evaluation-related consulting professions. She examines the ethical codes within evaluation and related disciplines and professions and discusses implications for content, dissemination, and compliance.*

# Ethics in Disciplines and Professions Related to Evaluation

*Jody L. Fitzpatrick*

Donald Campbell (1969) bemoaned the traditional isolation, or ethnocentrism, of different disciplines. Using the analogy of a fish, he presented a fish-scale model of omniscience in depicting the social sciences and related disciplines. Each discipline believes it knows the truth (the whole fish) when, in fact, we tend to know only our own discipline (single scale). This chapter is designed to help us avoid such ethnocentrism in ethical matters and instead, as Campbell argued we should, learn from related fields.

## Ethical Codes in Program Evaluation

To provide a foundation for this learning, I first briefly review the history of ethical codes in evaluation. In the early 1980s two documents were published to guide evaluators in their ethical considerations: the *Standards for Evaluations of Educational Programs, Projects, and Materials* (Joint Committee on Standards for Educational Evaluation, 1981) and the Evaluation Research Society (ERS) *Standards for Program Evaluation* (ERS Standards Committee, 1982). The first was initiated by the Joint Committee, which had representation from twelve sponsoring organizations primarily from the disciplines of education and psychology. Their focus was on the evaluation of educational programs, but the standards also had implications for evaluation in other settings (Stufflebeam, 1982). The ERS standards were the first to emerge from a professional association devoted solely to evaluation, the Evaluation Research Society.

The mid-1990s saw the publication of two newer documents of concern to ethics in evaluation. The first was a revision of the earlier standards (Joint Committee on Standards for Educational Evaluation, 1994). These standards maintained the same four major groups of standards—utility, feasibility, propriety, and accuracy—but within these major categories some of the original thirty standards were combined and others were revised. Further, these newer standards, *The Program Evaluation Standards,* were intended to address evaluations beyond the educational arena, though much of the focus remains on education and training. Similarly, in 1995, the American Evaluation Association (AEA) published its new *Guiding Principles for Evaluators.* These guiding principles offered a set of values—for example, honesty, integrity, and responsibility for public welfare—as guides for evaluation practice. (In 1986, the Evaluation Research Society had merged with Evaluation Network to form the American Evaluation Association, a professional association to represent the entire profession in the United States. AEA chose not to adopt the old ERS standards, but rather to develop its own guiding principles.) Today, evaluators in the United States have these two documents to advise their ethical practice. Other countries (Canada), organizations (Government Accounting Office), and groups of countries (Australasian Evaluation Society) have developed their own standards. (See Worthen, Sanders, and Fitzpatrick [1997] for a discussion of these.)

What can we learn from these two documents and from the history of ethical codes for evaluation? Comparing the documents published in the early 1980s with those published in the mid-1990s reveals a major change: a move to include a greater focus on non-methodological issues. This change is most obvious in comparing the ERS standards and the AEA guiding principles. Table 1.1 lists the major headings for both. The ERS standards generally mirror the stages of an evaluation. In contrast, the AEA guiding principles are more concerned with qualities or principles that permeate the evaluation process. As I discuss further on, the nature of the guiding principles is more congruent with the ethical codes of other professional associations. That is, the articulation of values, as opposed to stages of tasks, is a more common strategy in other ethical codes. Perhaps more important to the history of evaluation, this change mirrors the move in the education and training of evaluators from a very strong focus on methodological issues (which certainly remains the *sine qua non* of evaluation) to a greater examination of the many political factors and personal judgments entailed in conducting evaluations. This change has been positively noted in several of the commentaries on the AEA Guiding Principles with special reference

### Table 1.1. ERS Standards versus AEA Principles: Major Headings

| ERS Standards | AEA Principles |
|---|---|
| Formulation and negotiation | Systematic inquiry |
| Structure and design | Competence |
| Data collection and preparation | Integrity/honesty |
| Data analysis and interpretation | Respect for people |
| Communication and disclosure | Responsibilities for general |
| Utilization | and public welfare |

to the principle concerning responsibilities for the general and public welfare (E) (Covert, 1995; House, 1995).

Though the headings in Table 1.1 reflect changes in the tone and emphasis in evaluation ethics from the 1980s to the 1990s, the difference should not be overstated. As one might expect, the overlap between the entire body of ERS Standards and the AEA Guiding Principles is great; most of the topics and content covered in the first are reflected in the second. The converse is also true, even in controversial areas. The ERS Standards thus recommended identifying various groups of stakeholders and their "information needs and expectations" (ERS Standards Committee, 1982, p. 12). They even argued that "evaluators should also help identify areas of public interest in the program" (ERS Standards Committee, 1982, p. 12). But the tone is different. The AEA Guiding Principles emphasize the diverse groups we serve, or might serve, and our obligation to be inclusive in ensuring those groups are represented. Finally, the language used in major headings is important. One goal of professional codes is to inspire ethical behavior among its members. Lofty language can help in that regard. As such, the major categories for the AEA Guiding Principles, as with the Joint Committee Standards, are more inspirational than the step-by-step emphasis of the earlier ERS Standards.

## The Social Sciences and Evaluation Codes

The ethical codes discussed above have been strongly influenced by ethics concerning social science research in specific disciplines. This influence can be seen in the initial impetus for the codes and in their process of development. The original standards (1981) were a spinoff from the revision of the *Standards for Educational and Psychological Tests and Manuals* by the American Educational Research Association (AERA), the American Psychological Association (APA), and the National Council on Measurement in Education. The twelve sponsoring organizations for the 1994 version continue to represent these areas, but the validation panel for the newer Joint Committee Standards also included broader audiences to represent adult training in many areas. Nevertheless, the focus remained on education and training. The development of the AEA Guiding Principles was initiated by reviewing the ethical codes in psychology (APA), education (AERA), and anthropology (American Anthropology Association, AAA). The committee also reviewed other codes dealing with research, including the federal regulations on *Protection of Human Subjects* and the *Belmont Report* on biomedical and behavioral research (Shadish, Newman, Scheirer, and Wye, 1995).

These documents, which focus primarily on research, are certainly pertinent to the ethical principles of program evaluators. They provide important guidelines concerning the design of research and the ethical concerns entailed when one collects data from people. However, the almost exclusive focus on the social sciences fails to inform us of the ethical conflicts and issues faced by professions, such as evaluation, that work directly with clients. As I have argued elsewhere, because the graduate training of most evaluators is in the social sciences, we tend to use these *disciplines* as exemplars and neglect *professions* that are similar to our own (Fitzpatrick, 1994). As the AEA Guiding Principles introduce ethical issues concerning relationships with clients and the public, balancing of stakeholder needs, and the values involved in these interactions, the ethical codes of other professions that struggle with conflicts among clients, other stakeholders, the public welfare, and the values of their discipline become important learning tools. In fact, the Joint Committee has found some procedures from the accounting profession to be useful in developing their standards for evaluation (Sanders, 1999).

The AEA Guiding Principles were initiated to stimulate dialogue among program evaluators on how we deal with ethical dilemmas. Yet, that dialogue has not progressed as much as many might have desired. Some might argue that the absence of dialogue is due to the generality of the principles (Rossi, 1995). House writes that the "endorsement of general principles sometimes seems platitudinous or irrelevant" (1995, p. 27). However, he goes on to encourage the dialogue, observing that, "Ethical concerns become interesting only in conflicted cases, and it is often the balance of principles that is crucial rather than the principles themselves" (House, 1995, p. 27). Examining the codes, cases, and procedures of professions confronting similar conflicts can be fruitful in further stimulating this dialogue.

## Consulting versus Scholarly Professions

Bayles (1981), in writing about professional ethics as a broad subject, makes an important distinction between *consulting professionals* and *scholarly professionals*. Admitting the terms represent a continuum and the middle can become murky, Bayles writes that consulting professionals differ from scholarly professionals in two important ways: they establish personal, working relationships with their clients, and their method of reimbursement is typically fee-for-service. In contrast, scholarly professionals generally deal with clients at a distance (students in a class, readers of a journal) and are salaried. Consulting professionals work as "entrepreneurs" and, as such, "depend on attracting individual clients" (Bayles, 1981, p. 9). Consulting professionals include lawyers, physicians, architects, consulting engineers, accountants, and psychologists. Scholarly professionals include teachers, professors, and scientific researchers. As program evaluators who use research methods, we may fall in that murky middle, but I would argue that we are more akin to consulting engineers or accountants in our relationships with clients than we are to our social science brethren.

The different economic and personal relationships with clients, Bayles argues, "are crucial in defining the kinds of ethical problems each confronts" (1981, p. 9). The personal relationships that consulting professionals develop with their clients and the expectations engendered by clients' direct hiring and reimbursement of the professional can exacerbate many ethical dilemmas.

Because the relationship of the consulting professional is closer to the client than to other stakeholders, the professional must guard against bias toward, or overidentification with, the clients' views or needs. Further, because the professionals' ongoing livelihood depends on attracting and retaining clients, it can be against the professionals' self-interest (at least in the short-term) to pursue ethical norms that conflict with the clients' self-perceived needs. The scholarly professional is not so buffeted by the pressures of individual clients' expectations or the exigencies of maintaining a practice. This distinction can be useful for evaluators in considering ethical codes. Certainly, for methodological issues, our ethical codes should build on those from the scholarly professions. But as evaluation ethics moves toward a focus on the values entailed in dealing with diverse stakeholders and balancing the public interest, we can also look to the consulting professions for guidance.

## The Content of Various Professional Codes

Codes of professional groups vary considerably in their comprehensiveness, explicitness, and means of enforcement. Table 1.2 presents the principles of several professional associations, both scholarly and consulting. (These principles are referred to as standards, canons, and principles by the different groups, but they all represent the first level of values articulated in the code.) One first notices the commonality across principles in spite of the variation in the fields represented. Several (accounting, engineering, public administration) begin with a principle concerning the public service or public welfare. Psychology ends

**Table 1.2. A Sample of Characteristics of Selected Professional Codes**

| Profession | Principles* |
| --- | --- |
| Accounting (AICPA) | Responsibilities as professionals, serving the public interest, integrity, objectivity and independence, exercise due care, apply principles to scope and nature of services |
| Internal auditors (IAA) | Honesty, objectivity, diligence, loyalty, conflicts of interest, fees or gifts, confidentiality, due care to obtain sufficient factual evidence to support the expression of an opinion |
| Professional engineers (NSPE) | Safety, health, and welfare of the public; competence; objective and truthful; faithful agent of employer or client; avoid deceptive acts; conduct oneself honorably and responsibly to honor the profession |
| Psychology (APA) | Competence, integrity, professional and scientific responsibility, respect for people's rights and dignity, concern for others' welfare, social responsibility |
| Public administration (ASPA) | Serve public interest, respect constitution and law, integrity, promote ethical organizations, strive for professional excellence |

*The principles are listed in their order of presentation in the codes, because this order may reflect the priorities of the discipline or profession.

with a principle concerning social responsibilities. The prominence of attention to the public good in many of these codes may reflect the consulting profession's desire to emphasize explicitly and prominently the importance of audiences other than the direct client. Although the professional engineer's code includes a principle concerning serving as a faithful agent to a client or employer, their code, too, emphasizes, first and foremost, the obligation to the safety, health, and welfare of the public. The complete discussion of their canons, rules, and professional obligations stresses this priority. The American Institute of Certified Public Accountants (AICPA) expressly states, "In resolving those conflicts [between different audiences or stakeholders], members should act with integrity, guided by the precept that when members fulfill their responsibility to the public, clients' and employers' interests are best served" (Albrecht, 1992, p. 175). They define the public interest as "the collective well-being of the community of people and institutions the profession serves" (Albrecht, 1992, p. 175).

Of course, the role of accountants generally differs from that of program evaluators. But for many public accountants, their work in assessing a program and defining public interest might be quite similar to those of a program evaluator. (See Wisler [1996] for a discussion of the similarities and differences in the roles of auditors and evaluators.)

In contrast to these codes, which emphasize the professional's obligation to the *general* public, the AEA Guiding Principles stress the *diversity* of participants in the evaluation process and the need to recognize these differences, consider the interests of all groups, and provide results in such a way that they are accessible to all. The emphasis is on the heterogeneity of stakeholders, not the homogeneity. But the principles close with an exhortation to "encompass the public interest and good," which, they acknowledge, "are rarely the same as the interests of any particular group." This latter admonition more closely mirrors the codes of other associations. The committee, however, noted struggling with this issue, and as they acknowledge, further discussion and interpretation are needed to apply this principle effectively (Shadish and others, 1995). These other codes might provide some effective guidance.

As a frame for analysis, Bayles (1981) has identified six standards of a good or trustworthy professional: honesty, candor, competence, diligence, loyalty, and discretion. Most of these standards can be seen in the professional codes listed in Table 1.2 and in the AEA Guiding Principles shown in Table 1.1. Honesty is addressed in varying ways. It heads the list for internal auditors. Accountants and engineers stress "objectivity"; accountants add "independence" and evaluators add "integrity." Bayles sees "candor" as going beyond honesty to include full disclosure. The code of professional engineers addresses candor, for example, by articulating a professional's obligations to acknowledge errors to clients and to advise clients when a project will not be successful.

Similarly, competence is addressed in each of the professional codes, but under different words. Only the code of professional engineers, like the AEA Guiding Principles, directly uses the word "competence." Accounting and internal auditors emphasize "due care," which incorporates both diligence and competence. Psychology and public administration articulate principles concerning professional responsibilities and professional excellence.

Loyalty is concerned largely with the conflict between obligations to clients and responsibilities to others, including the profession. The conflicts faced by professionals in this area are partly addressed by the principles concerning public and professional responsibilities. Many professional codes deal extensively with loyalty. Several of these codes address conflicts of interest and independence of judgment. These issues are subsumed under loyalty because the client has an expectation that the professional they hire has revealed any potential conflicts of interest that would hinder their completing the work fairly and will, in fact, be able to provide an independent judgment on the issue of concern. Guiding Principle E.4 states the need to "maintain a balance between client needs and other needs." The evaluator is urged to "meet legitimate client needs whenever it is feasible and appropriate to do so," but the principle notes that when client interests conflict with other principles, "evaluators should explicitly identify and discuss the conflicts with the client and relevant stakeholders" (American Evaluation Association, 1995, p. 25).

Discretion is addressed less directly by most professional codes. The AEA Guiding Principles, as with the code of ethics for psychology, addresses the issue of confidentiality under "respect for people." But, the implication is that these people are participants in the evaluation, not the agency or client. What obligation does the evaluator have to the client in regard to confidentiality and discretion? Guiding Principle E.3 advocates broad dissemination of findings. Under what circumstances is such dissemination unethical? An accounting ethics case asks readers whether an accounting professor should use materials from an outside project in the classroom (Albrecht, 1992). If so, should the identity of the firm be disclosed? Although laws on public records may cast an evaluation report on a public program in a different light, what ethical obligations for discretion does an evaluator have? What loyalty does the evaluator have to the client? These are issues that should be discussed, further building on the similarities and the distinctions between our profession and those in related fields.

## Enforcement of Ethical Codes

Historically, most consulting professions have been self-regulating. As professions often come under some criticism for their failure to regulate, professional associations have established mechanisms for enforcement of the codes that the evaluation profession currently lacks. The American Psychological Association, many of whose members are practicing psychologists, the American Bar Association (ABA), the American Medical Association (AMA), the American Institute of Certified Public Accountants (AICPA), and the National Association of Social Workers (NASW) all have enforcement bodies. These committees answer questions, hear complaints, and issue disciplinary decisions or sanctions as appropriate. Their hearings and decisions help build case law for the interpretation of the ethical codes.

In contrast, enforcement mechanisms are typically absent from the professional associations of scholarly professions. For example, the American Educational Research Association (AERA), the American Anthropology Association (AAA), and even the American Society for Public Administration (ASPA) develop and disseminate their ethical codes but have not developed official mechanisms for enforcement. Plant (1998) discusses the reasons for the absence of external enforcement mechanisms for the ASPA code, drawing on extensive writings in public administration concerning ways to create ethical behavior. Some argue against even the codification of professional ethics, maintaining that practitioners should be their own moral reasoners (Rohr, 1978). ASPA, however, argues that codes are necessary to socialize and educate the practitioner about common standards, but that enforcement at the individual level is more appropriate than central enforcement. Organizations such as ASPA appear to believe that the development of "inner controls" will be more successful at engendering ethical behavior among members than the "external management of conduct" (Plant, 1998, p. 165).

The AEA Guiding Principles may not include enforcement mechanisms because of a belief in the success of inner controls; however, the more likely reason for their absence may be the need to reach consensus on the meaning and application of the principles, the continuing tensions among the diverse paradigms used in evaluation, and the relative newness of the evaluation profession. All of these factors create difficulties in developing and implementing enforcement mechanisms. As evaluation matures as a field and greater consensus is achieved on the appropriate methods and actions of evaluators, development of enforcement mechanisms may be reconsidered. They seem more appropriate to the self-regulating role of the consulting professions.

If AEA continues to use internal mechanisms to motivate ethical behavior among members, however, revisions of the code may consider the use of language to better achieve that goal. The style of ASPA's Code of Ethics is consistent with the purpose of instilling internal controls. The code is short; it could fit on one legal-size page. It articulates five broad principles with four to eight brief points explicating each. The words and language used in this code are designed to inspire and are less legalistic than the codes of the professional agencies that include enforcement. The AEA Guiding Principles make use of this format (principles with brief points), but the tone of the language, as noted by the authors, is more legalistic than the ASPA codes.

In the absence of formal committees delegated with enforcement powers, other means of educating members and enforcing codes of ethics do exist and must be used to encourage understanding and compliance. The National Society of Professional Engineers, which does not have an official enforcement body, uses its Board of Ethical Review to interpret ethical dilemmas submitted by engineers, public officials, and members of the public. They publish these cases on-line and in print with an index, sponsor an annual ethics contest in which members respond to a case, and disseminate a series of videotapes for students and professionals. AICPA, which does have an enforcement body, has also worked actively to raise the consciousness of accounting students and professionals about their codes. Membership in the organization is contingent upon acceptance of the Code of Professional Conduct. The association has produced and distributed a videotape, *It's Up to You*, describing the code and examining five case studies. Congressional criticism of accountants associated with the savings and loan fiasco in the 1980s stimulated these actions; the profession was aroused to attend to ethics and its public image (Mintz, 1992).

## The Future for Our Ethical Codes

Compared to the disciplines and professions reviewed here, program evaluation is quite new. The accounting profession in the United States celebrated its centennial a few years ago (Mintz, 1992). Physicians, engineers, and lawyers have been defining their professions and tinkering with their ethical codes for even longer. It is therefore not surprising that the ethical codes for program evaluators are less well formed; their state reflects the state of our field. However, we can learn from the codes reviewed here. A most immediate issue, which does not require consensus but instead action, is to continue to expand the dialogue that the AEA Guiding Principles were intended to create. We need more discussion of cases through our publications and conferences to argue and interpret the meaning of various principles. The publication of a new series in *The American Journal of Evaluation* on ethical challenges is a first step in that direction (Morris, 1998). EvalTalk and focus groups at the annual conference can be used to further articulate the meaning of various principles. I am currently working on a casebook for the American Evaluation Association, for which I will draw upon styles used in other professions. Current discussions of certification or licensure are pertinent to our ethical codes. Certification and licensure, as with accreditation, provide a mechanism for ensuring that professionals are informed of and concerned with our ethical codes. Finally, consideration might be given to linking membership in the American Evaluation Association with the AEA Guiding Principles. The Joint Committee Standards for Program Evaluation, AEA's Guiding Principles for Evaluators, and codes from other disciplines have provided us with food for thought. Now we must continue to discuss and articulate what it means to be an ethical evaluator.

## References

Albrecht, W. S. *Ethical Issues in the Practice of Accounting*. Cincinnati: South-Western, 1992.

American Evaluation Association. "Guiding Principles for Evaluators." In W. R. Shadish, D. L. Newman, M. A. Scheirer, and C. Wye (eds.), *Guiding Principles for Evaluators*. New Directions for Program Evaluation, no. 66. San Francisco: Jossey-Bass, 1995.

Bayles, M. D. *Professional Ethics*. Belmont, Calif.: Wadsworth, 1981.

Campbell, D. "Ethnocentrism of Disciplines and the Fish-Scale Model of Omniscience." In M. Sherif and C. Sherif (eds.), *Inter-disciplinary Relationships in the Social Sciences*. Chicago: Aldine, 1969.

Covert, R. W. "A Twenty-Year Veteran's Reflections on the Guiding Principles for Evaluators." In W. R. Shadish, D. L. Newman, M. A. Scheirer, and C. Wye (eds.), *Guiding Principles for Evaluators*. New Directions for Program Evaluation, no. 66. San Francisco: Jossey-Bass, 1995.

Evaluation Research Society (ERS) Standards Committee. "Evaluation Research Society Standards for Program Evaluation." In P. Rossi (ed.), *Standards for Evaluation Practice*. New Directions for Program Evaluation, no. 15. San Francisco: Jossey-Bass, 1982.

Fitzpatrick, J. L. "Alternative Models for the Structuring of Professional Preparation Programs." In J. W. Altschuld and M. Engle (eds.), *The Preparation of Professional Evaluators: Issues, Perspectives, and Programs*. New Directions for Program Evaluation, no. 62. San Francisco: Jossey-Bass, 1994.

House, E. R. "Principled Evaluation: A Critique of the AEA Guiding Principles." In W. R. Shadish, D. L. Newman, M. A. Scheirer, and C. Wye (eds.), *Guiding Principles for Evaluators*. New Directions for Program Evaluation, no. 66. San Francisco: Jossey-Bass, 1995.

Joint Committee on Standards for Educational Evaluation. *Standards for Evaluations of Educational Programs, Projects, and Materials*. New York: McGraw-Hill, 1981.

Joint Committee on Standards for Educational Evaluation. *The Program Evaluation Standards*. Second Edition. Thousand Oaks, Calif.: Sage, 1994.

Mintz, S. M. *Cases in Accounting Ethics and Professionalism*. New York: McGraw Hill, 1992.

Morris, M. "Ethical Challenges." *American Journal of Evaluation*, 1998, *19*, 381–382.

Plant, J. F. "Using Codes of Ethics in Teaching Public Administration." In J. Bowman and D. Menzel (eds.), *Teaching Ethics and Values in Public Administration Programs*. Albany, N.Y.: State University of New York Press, 1998.

Rohr, J. A. *Ethics for Bureaucrats: An Essay on Law and Values*. New York: Marcel Dekker, 1978.

Rossi, P. H. "Doing Good and Getting It Right." In W. R. Shadish, D. L. Newman, M. A. Scheirer, and C. Wye (eds.), *Guiding Principles for Evaluators*. New Directions for Program Evaluation, no. 66. San Francisco: Jossey-Bass, 1995.

Sanders, J. Personal communication, January, 1999.

Shadish, W. R., Newman, D. L., Scheirer, M. A., and Wye, C. (1995). "Developing the Guiding Principles." In W. R. Shadish, D. L. Newman, M. A. Scheirer, and C. Wye (eds.), *Guiding Principles for Evaluators*. New Directions for Program Evaluation, no. 66. San Francisco: Jossey-Bass, 1995.

Stufflebeam, D. L. "A Next Step: Discussion to Consider Unifying the ERS and Joint Committee Standards." In P. H. Rossi (ed.), *Standards for Evaluation Practice*. New Directions for Program Evaluation, no. 15. San Francisco: Jossey-Bass, 1982.

Wisler, C. (ed.). *Evaluation and Auditing: Prospects for Convergence*. New Directions for Evaluation, no. 71. San Francisco: Jossey-Bass, 1996.

Worthen, B. R., Sanders, J. R., and Fitzpatrick, J. L. *Program Evaluation*. New York: Longman, 1997.

*JODY L. FITZPATRICK is associate professor of public administration at the University of Colorado. She maintains an active practice in evaluation and is interested in the ethical nuances of evaluator-client relations. She serves on the Board of the American Evaluation Association and is working on a book of case studies for the Association.*

*Although empirical research on evaluation ethics is not plentiful, several important findings have emerged. These include an apparent lack of consensus within the field concerning what constitutes an ethical issue, the frequent occurrence of ethical problems during the later stages of evaluation projects, and the perceived ethical significance of the tendency for evaluators to be more responsive to some stakeholders than others. The author discusses the need to incorporate research questions on ethics into ongoing evaluation projects and to assess systematically evaluators' perceptions of AEA's Guiding Principles.*

# Research on Evaluation Ethics: What Have We Learned and Why Is It Important?

*Michael Morris*

Nearly twenty years ago Sheinfeld and Lord (1981) noted that "empirical studies of the ethical concerns of evaluation researchers are few" (p. 380). What was true then is only slightly less true today. Indeed, at a recent session devoted to "What Should We Be Researching in Evaluation Ethics?" (Morris, 1997) at the American Evaluation Association's (AEA's) annual meeting, the panelists outnumbered the audience! Whatever else ethical issues may be, they do not appear to have attracted the attention of a large segment of the research community in evaluation.

This is not to say, of course, that there has been virtual silence on the subject beyond the *Guiding Principles for Evaluators* and the Joint Committee's *Program Evaluation* Standards. Analyses of ethical concerns, frequently based on the personal experiences of the authors, are relatively easy to find (see English, 1997; Gensheimer, Ayers, and Roosa, 1993; Schwandt, 1997; Stake and Mabry, 1998). Far fewer, however, are cases in which the authors have gathered primary data in a systematic fashion for the explicit purpose of shedding light on ethical issues in evaluation. In a field that prides itself on being committed to decision making informed by such data, this state of affairs is cause for concern. Accordingly, this chapter will focus on primary-data studies and their value for enhancing our understanding of evaluation ethics.

## Evaluators' Experiences with Ethical Challenges

Two of the most fundamental questions that ethics researchers can attempt to answer are (1) *to what extent* do evaluators see themselves as encountering ethical problems in their work, and (2) *what types* of problems do they encounter?

**Pervasiveness of Ethical Problems.** The answer to the first question is perhaps surprising. In a 1991 survey of AEA members, Morris and Cohn (1993) found that 35 percent of their 459 respondents said "no" when they were asked, "In your work as a program evaluator, have you ever encountered an ethical problem or conflict to which you had to respond?" Individuals in the "no" group had conducted fewer evaluations, had devoted more of their time to internal evaluation, and were more likely to have been trained in the field of education than respondents who reported that they *had* encountered ethical conflicts in their work.

Although we were initially taken aback by the substantial size of the "no" group, the findings of other researchers appear to be generally consistent with ours. When summarizing their program of research on evaluation ethics, Newman and Brown (1996) observe: "We consistently found people whose generalized response was 'What? Ethics? What does ethics have to do with evaluation?' This came from experienced evaluators, long-term users of evaluation, evaluation interns, and faculty members teaching evaluation" (p. 89). Even more striking are the results of Honea's (1992) in-depth interviews of nine evaluators in the public sector. Although a major purpose of her study was to identify and describe the ethical issues and dilemmas encountered by these evaluators, Honea found that "ethics was not discussed during the practice of evaluation and ethical dilemmas were rarely, if ever, identified during the conduct of evaluation and policy analysis activities" (p. 317).

At the very least, these findings suggest that there is a substantial subgroup of evaluators who are not inclined to interpret the challenges they face in ethical terms. A key question thus presents itself: Why do some evaluators view certain types of work-related problems through an ethical lens, whereas others do not? One factor that may be operating here is whether the evaluator is functioning primarily in an internal or an external role. Recall that Morris and Cohn found that internal evaluators were less likely than external ones to report that they had ever faced an ethical conflict. Mathison (1991) has suggested that internal evaluators are especially vulnerable to co-optation due to the role conflicts associated with being both a professional evaluator and a member of the organization being evaluated. Given that "organizations work against self-reflection and self-criticism" (p. 177), internal evaluators may work in an environment that encourages them not to question circumstances that outsiders might be inclined to see as ethically troublesome.

The internal-external distinction, however, can hardly represent the whole story in accounting for differences in "ethical sensitivity," since nearly half of the internal evaluators in Morris and Cohn's study indicated that they *had* experienced ethical conflicts, and nearly one-third of the external evaluators claimed that they had not. Honea (1992) has identified three additional factors worthy of consideration based on her interviews. She has labeled them the *objective scientist,* the *assumption of ethics,* and the *team,* and believes that these "themes" function in a way that reduces the likelihood of evaluators' perceiving and discussing the challenges they face in ethical terms.

Evaluators who endorse the *objective scientist* theme strive to be objective, fair, and impartial in their work. The evaluative goal here is to discover the truth and report it, and being an *ethical* evaluator means being an *objective* evaluator. Such an orientation can reduce the salience of ethics in at least two ways. First, it appears that Honea's interviewees viewed themselves as quite successful in their attempts to achieve objectivity on the job. This success minimizes the perceived occurrence of ethical incidents in their lives as evaluators. Second, when deviations from objectivity *are* encountered, the "response hierarchy" of these evaluators predisposes them to regard the occurrences as *methodological* or *political* challenges rather than ethical ones (see Morris, 1998, p. 381).

The *assumption of ethics* refers to the belief that "everyone understands the ethical expectations that are part of the profession and the organization" (Honea, 1992, p.303), hence there is little need for discussion of ethical issues. At first glance it may not be clear how this assumption obviates the need to discuss ethical problems posed by the behavior of stakeholders who do not share these values. However, some evaluators may regard their responses to these problems as taking place at an intuitive level that does not require deliberation. Bonnet (1998), for example, has claimed that an evaluator's decision "not to lie (or misrepresent by omission) in the interest of client service is too reflexive a choice to constitute a dilemma [of ethics]" (p. 231). In essence, she is arguing that certain situations are so unequivocal in terms of how the evaluator should respond that they do not represent genuine ethical dilemmas. The assumption of ethics thus serves the evaluation community in much the same, unobtrusive way that Adam Smith's "invisible hand" benefits the economy.

Finally, Honea's respondents believed that being part of an evaluation *team* helped to *prevent* unethical behavior from occurring. Team meetings and discussions provide evaluators with the opportunity to perform a "checks and balances" function with respect to their fellow team members' biases and blind spots, thus reducing the likelihood that ethical blunders will be made in the course of an evaluation.

The extent to which the explanations posited by Honea can be generalized beyond her small sample of public sector evaluators is an important question for future investigators to explore. Whatever path this research follows, the findings summarized in this section point to a reality that the field can ill afford to ignore, a reality in which the perceived salience and significance of ethical concerns vary dramatically among the members of the profession.

**The Nature of Ethical Challenges.**  Our focus now shifts to those who *have* reported ethical conflicts in their work. In the Morris and Cohn study, respondents were asked in an open-ended question to describe the "ethical problems or conflicts you have encountered most frequently in your work as an evaluator."

They were also asked to describe the most serious ethical problem they had faced. Among the 290 evaluators who reported at least one problem in responding to the first question, conflicts involving the *presentation of evaluation findings* were, by far, the most frequently described. Nearly 60 percent of the respondents presented problems that fit into this category. (This was also deemed the *most serious* conflict area by the greatest number [47 percent] of respondents.) Within this general category, the specific problem most often reported was that of being pressured by a stakeholder—usually the primary client—to slant one's presentation of the findings in a direction favored by the stakeholder.

A significant number of respondents (from 22 to 28 percent) also indicated that they frequently had to deal with ethical dilemmas involving misinterpretation and misuse of evaluation results, identifying and clarifying the needs of stakeholders, and adhering to disclosure agreements. The specific conflicts most likely to be encountered in these areas involved findings being suppressed or ignored by a key stakeholder; stakeholders whose behavior during the contracting phase suggested that they had already decided what the findings "should be" or that they had plans to use the findings in an ethically questionable fashion; occasions where confidentiality of data sources might be compromised due to stakeholder pressure or the presence of identifying characteristics in the evaluation report; and disputes or uncertainties concerning ownership and distribution of the final report, raw data, and so forth.

It is instructive to compare Morris and Cohn's results with the problems reported by Honea's (1992) respondents. Although Honea's sample did not indicate that ethical dilemmas were pervasive in their work, the characteristic shared by most of the challenges they *did* describe involved "telling the *truth* as identified by the evaluation study despite political pressures to do otherwise" (p. 280). One of her respondents described the dilemma as "coming into projects where your client already has the answer and is asking you to justify a conclusion. So the ethical dilemma is do you tell them the truth or do you tell them what they want to hear" (p. 280). This theme bears a striking resemblance to the ethical conflict that Morris and Cohn's sample mentioned most frequently: being pressured to report evaluation findings in a distorted fashion.

A different method for investigating evaluators' perceptions of ethical conflicts has been used by Newman and Brown (1996). In their survey studies, statements representing violations of the Joint Committee's *Program Evaluation Standards* were presented to respondents, who were asked to indicate how frequently these violations occurred, and how serious they were. Table 2.1 presents the results from their sample of practicing evaluators. The violation that received the highest ranking for frequency was "Evaluator selects a test primarily because of his or her familiarity with it." Program administrators and program staff in Newman and Brown's sample also ranked this violation as the most frequently occurring one in evaluation. The only other violation that was ranked high in frequency by all three groups was "Evaluation responds to the concerns of one interest group more than another's."

The violation that evaluators ranked as most serious was "Evaluator changes the evaluation questions to match the data analysis." There was a great deal of sim-

### Table 2.1.  Evaluators' Perceptions of Most Frequent and Most Serious Violations

| Most Frequent | Most Serious |
| --- | --- |
| Evaluator selects a test primarily because of his or her familiarity with it. | Evaluator changes the evaluation questions to match the data analysis. |
| Evaluator loses interest in the evaluation when the final report is delivered. | Evaluator promises confidentiality when it cannot be guaranteed. |
| Evaluation responds to the concerns of one interest group more than another. | Evaluator makes decisions without consulting with the client when consultation has been agreed to. |
| Evaluator fails to find out what the values are of right-to-know audiences. | Evaluator conducts an evaluation when he or she lacks sufficient skills or experience. |
| Evaluator writes a highly technical report for a technically unsophisticated audience. | Evaluation report is written so that partisan interest groups can delete embarrassing weaknesses. |

*Source*: Adapted from Newman and Brown, 1996.

ilarity in the violations selected as most serious by all three groups of respondents. Evaluators and program staff placed the same five violations at the top of their lists, whereas evaluators and program administrators had four out of five in common.

Given the different methodologies employed in the Morris and Cohn and Newman and Brown studies, it is not surprising that their overall results differ. Morris and Cohn's survey was open-ended and focused on evaluators' *personal* encounters with ethical conflicts. Newman and Brown generated a list of thirty ethical violations, with phrasing that emphasized the *evaluator's* responsibility for the problem, and asked respondents for their perceptions of the incidence and frequency of these offenses within the evaluation field *as a whole*. The results of the two investigations can thus be seen as pertaining to related but distinct domains. Morris and Cohn are soliciting evaluators' "ethical autobiographies," personal accounts that usually absolve the narrator of responsibility for the problem faced. Indeed, the tendency not to see oneself as the source of one's problems is a phenomenon well documented in research on attributional processes (see Jones and others, 1971). Newman and Brown, however, are interested in evaluators' at-a-distance perspective on violations committed within the overall evaluation community, a perspective that may be less likely than autobiographical accounts to be affected by self-serving perceptions. And recall that the Newman and Brown focus is on *actual* violations of ethical practice, rather than on problems that might—or might not—*lead to* such violations (the Morris and Cohn focus), depending on how the parties involved address the situation. Against this background, to claim that one set of findings is more accurate than the other is probably ill-advised. An appreciation of both is necessary to achieve a full understanding of practitioners' views of the ethical minefield that evaluation can represent.

**Studies of Specific Ethical Issues.** The research just reviewed surveys evaluators' experiences with a wide range of ethical challenges. There are also a small number of investigations that have gathered data on a particular ethical concern as an actual evaluation has evolved. Heflinger, Nixon, and Hamner (1996), for example, examined the impact of a standardized process for disclosing confidential information to parents, service providers, or state authorities that was used during the evaluation of the Fort Bragg Child and Adolescent Mental Health Demonstration (Bickman, 1996). The process was developed to assist evaluation staff in determining whether risks involving abuse, suicide, or serious harm toward others existed in the lives of the program's clients. The application of this process throughout the evaluation led to disclosure of confidential information on less than 5 percent of the clients in the Demonstration. Not surprisingly, this small subgroup of clients was found to be significantly more psychologically impaired than the other clients in the program. The disclosure of confidential information did not appear to have a negative impact on the willingness of clients' families to continue participating in the evaluation. Overall, the results suggest that it is possible to develop standardized methods for dealing with at least some of the ethical challenges involving confidentiality and disclosure that occur in mental health evaluations.

Another line of research has targeted the issue of active versus passive parental consent in research on minors. Active consent requires parents to return a consent form in order for the child to participate in a study, whereas passive consent only requires parents to return the form if they do *not* wish for their child to participate. Although the need to obtain informed consent is an ethical imperative widely acknowledged among evaluators (see AEA principle (D), "respect for people"), controversy surrounds legislative attempts to require various forms of active consent (see Renger, Gotkin, Crago, and Shisslak, 1998). This is because procedures for active consent generally produce lower participation rates than passive ones, thus posing a serious threat to the representativeness of samples obtained through the former approach (see Ellickson and Hawes, 1989; Esbensen and others, 1996; Lueptow, Mueller, Hammes, and Master, 1977; Severson and Biglan, 1989). To the extent that these lower participation rates are due to parental *apathy* rather than genuine parental *opposition* to the study or the program, the ethical advantage of active methods over passive ones in obtaining informed consent would seem to be lessened. The evidence is mixed, however, regarding the relative impact of these two factors in explaining parental noncooperation when active methods are employed (Esbensen and others, 1996; Lueptow and others, 1977).

One of the lessons that has emerged from these investigations is that intensive follow-up procedures (for example, repeat mailings, phone calls, parents' meetings) can significantly enhance participation rates in active-consent situations (Ellickson and Hawes, 1989). However, this approach requires evaluators to establish an excellent working relationship with administrators and staff in the program setting and to have access to substantial resources in terms of time, money, and research personnel.

Finally, ethnographic approaches have been used to explore ethical issues in ongoing evaluations. Lam, Hartwell, and Jekel (1994), for example, interviewed clients (treatment and control), community service providers, and research staff to determine their reactions to randomization in a demonstration project providing residential, case-management, and other services to homeless male substance abusers. They found that, overall, clients in the control group reacted less negatively to being randomly assigned to "usual care" than the service providers and research staff had feared. In contrast, the providers and research staff were more negative in their emotional responses to the randomization process than the researchers had anticipated. Indeed, the task of implementing randomization generated significant strains in the relationship between service providers and research staff throughout much of the evaluation. The results of this study underscore the importance of sensitively managing the expectations of multiple stakeholders when using methodologies that are likely to cause ethical controversy.

## Research on Values, Standards, Principles, and Roles

The evaluation community's attempts to articulate its values and develop standards to guide its work have been the subject of a cluster of studies. In one of the earliest such investigations, Sheinfeld and Lord (1981) asked a sample of evaluators to rate the importance of, and their support for, forty-seven ethical statements pertaining to evaluation practice. The results indicated that respondents felt strongly about three general domains: protection of human subjects, freedom from political interference, and evaluators' technical competency. In discussing their findings, the authors speculated that evaluators' commitment to *distributive justice* as a core value might significantly increase as the field evolved. Indeed, approaches such as empowerment, advocacy, and participatory evaluation have received attention in recent years, thus seeming to support this prediction.

DeBrey (1989) surveyed and interviewed a small sample of researchers to ascertain how applicable they thought the Evaluation Research Society (ERS) standards were to specific evaluation projects they had conducted. The respondents voiced several major criticisms of the standards. Some standards were seen as "truisms" of little distinctive use to evaluators. Problems with conflicting or redundant standards were also reported. Certain standards were seen as inappropriately rigid, and many of them were regarded as being strongly biased toward quantitative, experimental research. Closely related to this criticism was the view that the different value orientations and models that characterize the evaluation field were not sufficiently acknowledged in the standards.

Although the ERS standards are no longer cited frequently in discussions of evaluation ethics, DeBrey's research remains relevant. His findings highlight the challenges that any set of evaluation standards or principles must successfully address if they are to be perceived as useful by practitioners.

A similar contribution is made by McKillip and Garberg's (1986) research on the Joint Committee Standards. Based on evaluators' ratings of each of the thirty standards on a variety of scales, the researchers statistically derived five clusters of standards representing the following evaluation tasks:

• Attending to the contextual and political dimensions of the evaluation
• Displaying professionalism
• Conducting the evaluation openly and consulting widely
• Abiding by the canons of social science practice
• Tailoring the research design to the specific evaluation setting

The results further suggest that dealing with an evaluation's contextual and political factors—the task defined by the first cluster of standards—is the activity most likely to put the evaluator in conflict with the standards in the other clusters.

Finally, Newman and Brown (1996) have recently provided a detailed summary of a series of studies they conducted to examine evaluators' and stakeholders' views of how five ethical principles (autonomy, nonmaleficence, beneficence, justice, and fidelity) are related to the Joint Committee Standards, to examples of good and bad evaluation practice, and to three roles (administrator, researcher, reporter) typically occupied by evaluators. Although a review of these findings is beyond the scope of this chapter, at least three major themes that have emerged from this work should be noted. First, evaluators regard the principles of nonmaleficence (that is, do no harm), beneficence, and justice as being addressed by a sizeable number of the Joint Committee Standards. In contrast, very few standards are viewed by evaluators as being associated with autonomy and fidelity. Second, evaluators believe that their administrative, research, and reporting roles are reflected broadly in the standards. Finally, the views of stakeholders (that is, program administrators, staff, and participants) on these issues overlap, but are distinct from, those of evaluators.

## Conclusion

What lessons should evaluators derive from the research reviewed in this chapter? Five would seem to be noteworthy.

*Lesson 1.* We should recognize that the existence of the AEA Guiding Principles and the Joint Committee Standards does not mean there is a consensus among evaluators about what constitutes an ethical issue. Disagreement abounds. (For a vivid example, compare Bonnet [1998] and Schwandt [1998].) Further, it can be argued that disagreement at such a fundamental level represents a formidable obstacle to the maturation of evaluation as a profession. Much work remains to be done in exploring the nature of this disagreement and the strategies that might be used for addressing it.

*Lesson 2.* Evaluators should prepare carefully for the "end game" in evaluation projects. Of the ethical conflicts that Morris and Cohn's respondents encountered most frequently, three of them—problems with presentation of findings, misinterpretation and misuse of results, and difficulties with disclosure agreement—typically manifest themselves during the later stages of the evaluation. Paradoxically, *preventing* these conflicts is probably best accomplished during the evaluation's contracting phase.

*Lesson 3.* We should acknowledge the potential ethical significance of our tendency to be more responsive to some stakeholders than others in our evaluations, especially in view of findings indicating that stakeholders' perceptions can vary widely and conflict with one another (see Mercier, 1997). Acknowledging a reality, of course, is not synonymous with solving a problem, and working effectively with multiple stakeholders is probably one of the most difficult tasks in evaluation. Fortunately, those who wish to develop their abilities in this domain can draw upon an expanding literature of research and commentary (see Brandon, 1998; Whitmore, 1998).

*Lesson 4.* Much can be learned from incorporating research questions on ethics into *ongoing* evaluation projects. Doing this, of course, requires preliminary analysis of the ethical concerns most likely to be raised by the evaluation. Although the resources needed to investigate these questions comprehensively might be substantial in many cases, relatively "inexpensive" methodologies such as stakeholder interviews could enable even modest studies to yield significant benefits.

*Lesson 5.* The time has arrived for evaluators' perceptions of the AEA Guiding principles to be assessed systematically. The developers of the guiding principles asserted that "these principles are part of an evolving process of self-examination by the profession and should be revisited on a regular basis" (American Evaluation Association, 1995, p. 22). Past research on the ERS Standards and the Joint Committee Standards has increased our understanding of the core dimensions and problems that characterize aspirational statements in evaluation. This knowledge should be applied when designing approaches for reviewing the AEA Guiding Principles. Enlisting the methodological expertise of our field on behalf of the values we embrace represents one of the most worthwhile agendas for researchers in evaluation ethics.

## References

American Evaluation Association, Task Force on Guiding Principles for Evaluators. "Guiding Principles for Evaluators." In W. R. Shadish, D. L. Newman, M. A. Scheirer, and C. Wye (eds.), *Guiding Principles for Evaluators.* New Directions for Program Evaluation, no. 66. San Francisco: Jossey-Bass, 1995.

Bickman, L. "A Continuum of Care: More Is Not Always Better." *American Psychologist,* 1996, *51,* 689–701.

Bonnet, D. G. "Commentary: Achieving the Untroubled Slumber." *American Journal of Evaluation,* 1998, *19,* 230–232.

Brandon, P. R. "Stakeholder Participation for the Purpose of Helping Ensure Evaluation Validity: Bridging the Gap Between Collaborative and Non-collaborative Evaluations." *American Journal of Evaluation,* 1998, *19,* 325–337.

DeBrey, J. H. C. "Field Testing the Standards for Program Evaluation of the Evaluation Research Society." *Impact Assessment Bulletin,* 1989, *7,* (2, 3), 39–53.

Ellickson, P. L., and Hawes, J. A. "An Assessment of Active Versus Passive Methods of Obtaining Parental Consent." *Evaluation Review,* 1989, *13,* 45–55.

English, B. "Conducting Ethical Evaluations with Disadvantaged and Minority Target Groups." *Evaluation Practice,* 1997, *18,* 49–54.

Esbensen, F., and others. "Active Parental Consent in School-Based Research: An Examination of Ethical and Methodological Issues." *Evaluation Review*, 1996, *20*, 737–753.

Gensheimer, L. K., Ayers, T. S., and Roosa, M. K. "School-Based Preventive Interventions for At-Risk Populations: Practical and Ethical Issues." *Evaluation and Program Planning*, 1993, *16*, 159–167.

Heflinger, C. A., Nixon, C. T., and Hamner, K. "Handling Confidentiality and Disclosure in the Evaluation of Client Outcomes in Managed Mental Health Services for Children and Adolescents." *Evaluation and Program Planning*, 1996, *19*, 175–182.

Honea, G. E. *Ethics and Public Sector Evaluators: Nine Case Studies.* Unpublished doctoral dissertation, University of Virginia, 1992.

Jones, E. G., and others. *Attribution: Perceiving the Causes of Behavior.* Morristown, N.J.: General Learning Press, 1971.

Lam, J. A., Hartwell, S. W., and Jekel, J. F. "'I Prayed Real Hard, So I Know I'll Get In': Living with Randomization." In K. Conrad (ed.), *Critically Evaluating the Role of Experiments.* New Directions for Program Evaluation, no. 63. San Francisco: Jossey-Bass, 1994.

Lueptow, L., Mueller, S. A., Hammes, R. R., and Master, L. R. "The Impact of Informed Consent Regulations on Response Rate and Response Bias." *Social Methods and Research*, 1977, *6*, 183–204.

Mathison, S. "Role Conflicts for Internal Evaluators." *Evaluation and Program Planning*, 1991, *14*, 173–179.

McKillip, J., and Garberg, R. "Demands of the Joint Committee's Standards for Educational Evaluation." *Evaluation and Program Planning*, 1986, *9*, 325–333.

Mercier, C. "Participation in Stakeholder-Based Evaluation: A Case Study." *Evaluation and Program Planning*, 1997, *20*, 467–475.

Morris, M. (chair). "What Should We Be Researching in Evaluation Ethics?" Session presented at the American Evaluation Association conference, San Diego, November 1997.

Morris, M. "Ethical Challenges." *American Journal of Evaluation*, 1998, *19*, 381–382.

Morris, M., and Cohn, R. "Program Evaluators and Ethical Challenges: A National Survey." *Evaluation Review*, 1993, *17*, 621–642.

Newman, D. L., and Brown, R. D. *Applied Ethics for Program Evaluation.* Thousand Oaks, Calif.: Sage, 1996.

Renger, R., Gotkin, V., Crago, M., and Shisslak, C. "Research and Legal Perspectives on the Implications of the Family Privacy Protection Act for Research and Evaluation Involving Minors." *American Journal of Evaluation*, 1998, *19*, 191–202.

Schwandt, T. A. "The Landscape of Values in Evaluation: Charted Terrain and Unexplored Territory." In D. Rog and D. Fournier (eds.), *Progress and Future Directions in Evaluation: Perspectives on Theory, Practice, and Methods.* New Directions for Evaluation, no. 76. San Francisco: Jossey-Bass, 1997.

Schwandt, T. A. "Commentary: Moral Demands and Strong Evaluation." *American Journal of Evaluation*, 1998, *19*, 227–229.

Severson, H., and Biglan, A. "Rationale for the Use of Passive Consent Procedures in Smoking Prevention Research: Politics, Policy, and Pragmatics." *Preventive Medicine*, 1989, *18*, 267–279.

Sheinfeld, S. N., and Lord, G. L. "Ethics of Evaluation Researchers: An Exploration of Value Choices." *Evaluation Review*, 1981, *5*, 377–391.

Stake, R., and Mabry, L. "Ethics in Program Evaluation." *Scandinavian Journal of Social Welfare*, 1998, *7*, 99–109.

Whitmore, E. (ed.). *Understanding and Practicing Participatory Evaluation.* New Directions for Evaluation, no. 80. San Francisco: Jossey-Bass, 1998.

MICHAEL MORRIS *is professor of psychology and director of graduate field training in community psychology at the University of New Haven. He edits the column "Ethical Challenges" in the* American Journal of Evaluation.

*Internal and external evaluators experience the same ethical
dilemmas, and both work toward resolving them in principled, justified
ways. The different communities they occupy, however, affect how they
are likely to resolve their ethical dilemmas.*

# Rights, Responsibilities, and Duties: A Comparison of Ethics for Internal and External Evaluators

*Sandra Mathison*

All evaluators probably try to adhere to a common set of ethical principles, such as the American Evaluation Association's *Guiding Principles for Evaluators* or *The Program Evaluation Standards,* and both internal and external evaluators are as likely (or unlikely) to engage in ethical evaluation practice. Although many discussions of internal-external evaluation revolve around questions about objectivity, bias, and credibility, I will adopt the assumption (based primarily on a lack of evidence in the literature to indicate otherwise) that neither internal nor external evaluators are inherently more or less objective, biased, or credible. Therefore, the differences that will be highlighted in this chapter are issues related to the ethics of the situation (evaluating from inside or outside) and the attention evaluators pay to the ethics of the evaluand. Most determinations of what is a right thing to do or a right way to be are made situationally, and the situations for internal and external evaluators are different. Internal and external evaluators occupy different "communities" and it is the nature of those communities that is critical for considering the resolution of ethical dilemmas.

The first section of the chapter will examine the question of whether the ethical dilemmas faced by internal and external evaluators are themselves different. The second section will examine the details of situational differences based on the conclusion from the previous section that, in fact, most, if not all, ethical dilemmas are common to all evaluators. I will argue that given a backdrop of common ethical principles for evaluation practice, a community framework helps us to understand the differences between internal and external evaluators. In writing this chapter I have relied on existing research on internal-external evaluation and ethics, although it should be noted that the research base is limited. So this chapter should also be considered an attempt to take what we do know about ethics and the internal-external distinction and build a theoretical framework from that, which itself requires further examination and empirical testing.

## Are Ethical Dilemmas Different for Internal and External Evaluators?

The short answer to this question is no. There seems to be no concrete evidence in the literature to support the contention that the nature of ethical dilemmas differs depending on whether one is an internal or external evaluator. Although internal evaluators are less likely to report encountering ethical challenges, when they do, these challenges are not substantially different in kind from those reported by external evaluators (Morris and Cohn, 1993). Many ethical dilemmas stem from conflicting values over goals, processes, outcomes (Smith, 1985), and theoretical frameworks (Kirkhart, 1985), but these dimensions do not distinguish internal from external evaluators.

Still, there is a persistent view that ethical challenges for internal evaluators are unique. Adams (1985) suggests internal evaluators might encounter (1) pressure to downplay negative and emphasize positive findings, (2) valuing of routine, nonthreatening evaluation activities, (3) interest in having an evaluation unit but not in using evaluation results, or (4) reduced access to privileged information. Internal evaluations are suspect because, it is presumed, they can be manipulated more easily by administrators to justify decisions or pressured to present positive findings for public relations purposes (House, 1986). Some suggest that these latter two problems may be reduced if the client for the internal evaluation is sufficiently distant from both the evaluand and the evaluator within the organization, that is, is high enough in the hierarchy such that the "truth" is what matters most (Worthen, Sanders, and Fitzpatrick, 1997; see especially Chapter Twelve).

External evaluators also work with clients who may make an undue attempt to shape the design, execution, and reporting of the evaluation. Scriven (1983) posits a managerial ideology that describes, in general, the propensity for evaluators and evaluations to attend disproportionately to the interests and needs of program managers. This is not more or less the case for internal or external evaluators, although there is evidence that internal evaluators typically respond to decision makers' needs and try to increase the usability of evaluation information by decision makers (Love, 1983; Mathison, 1991a; Patton, 1997; Reavy, Littell, Gonda, and O'Neill, 1993; Winberg, 1991). However, many external evaluators operate within this ideology as well.

Additionally, symbolic uses of evaluation are not limited to either external or internal evaluations, although the symbolic nature of the evaluation might be more apparent to internal evaluators. For example, internal evaluators may be directly asked for public relations information to support a program, but external evaluators are often employed to obtain information to be used in seeking an extension of or application for funding. All programs have the potential for ethical or unethical practices, and all clients and evaluations done for them have the potential for ethical and unethical practices. And both internal and external evaluators serve masters who control their fates in some way, to some degree.

Perhaps an illustration of precisely the same ethical dilemma I have encountered as both an internal and external evaluator will illustrate the commonality of such dilemmas. In both roles I have been involved in evaluations of teacher development projects, projects frequently of modest duration and likely to have limited, specific impact on the teachers involved. In both situations I have been pressured (even ordered) to examine student outcomes from these projects. Politically and ideologically, to establish positive student outcomes is perceived to be the best evidence that teacher development was successful. In both the internal and external evaluation, this demand was unwarranted, given the limited nature of the interventions and the conceptualizations underlying them. This one example is not meant as a definitive counter-example, but it is typical of my experience as an evaluator.

The difference lies, then, not in the dilemmas, but in the ways in which they are resolved, which will be taken up in the next section. Internal and external evaluators do work under different conditions, operate within different communities, and therefore approach ethical dilemmas in potentially different ways.

## Understanding the Situational Differences of Internal and External Evaluators

Internal and external evaluators occupy different communities in their work as evaluators. Figure 3.1 situates internal and external evaluators with respect to organizations, the larger discipline or product context within which organizations operate, and the evaluation profession. Each of the spheres can be thought of as a community, not in the sense of place, but in the sense of "a shared commitment to a set of core values" (Etzioni, 1996, p. 13), or what Dewey referred to as "a mode of associated living, of conjoint communicated experience" (1916, p. 87). Communities are made up of individuals (like evaluators) exercising individual rights, responsibilities, and interests, as well as the rights, responsibilities, and interests of the community as a whole. For all evaluators, ethical behavior is a balance of personal integrity, personal interest, and community interest. As will be discussed further, internal evaluators have fewer communities within which they operate, but they are very closely tied to those communities. External evaluators have a wider array of communities within which they function, and although they no doubt have close ties with one (or more) of those communities it is less likely to be the community or organization within which the program they evaluate is situated. Neither of these circumstances has moral, political, or methodological superiority; they are simply different.

Internal evaluators work within a particular organization that is itself embedded in a larger context that is composed of similar and related organizations. So, for example, an internal evaluator might be employed by the Rivet and Staple Company, which is one of many organizations that does light manufacturing. Or an internal evaluator might be employed by the Caring and Giving Foundation, which is part of the larger context of not-for-profit charitable foundations.

External evaluators, however, may work across a number of organizations and perhaps across a number of different discipline or product contexts as well. For example, an external evaluator might be a faculty member at Big Time University and simultaneously be doing an evaluation study for the Neighborhood Elementary School, which is part of the larger context of American public schools, and an evaluation for the Boys and Girls Club, which is part of the larger context of not-for-profit social-service delivery systems. Both internal and external evaluators are part of the evaluation profession evidenced by their membership in professional associations, subscriptions to professional journals, and so on.

A critical difference between internal and external evaluators is this definition of community; internal evaluators are more oriented to communities consistent with their workplaces, whereas external evaluators are oriented to a diverse array of communities, including, but not limited to, the professional evaluation community, their academic discipline, employers (such as universities or consulting firms), funding agencies, local business communities, and so on. For internal evaluators, this community is defined first and foremost by the *organization* within which she is working, as well as the discipline or product context of which that organization is part. The evaluation profession is, then, just one piece of this mix. The internal evaluator has a role to play in each of these areas, roles that may conflict with one another (Mathison, 1991b). So the community for an internal evaluator begins with the organization and moves out to the discipline or product community and the evaluation profession. The ethical dilemmas encountered by an internal evaluator are situated specifically and particularly within the organization and involve people the evaluator knows and works with routinely. The most enduring element of the internal evaluator's community is the organization.

The community in which the external evaluator operates is not as clearly defined, because the particular organizations and even disciplines in which he works are changeable. The ethical dilemmas encountered by an external evaluator are situational, occur in a changing work environment, and involve people the evaluator may or may not know and does not work with routinely. The primary community for an external evaluator is less predictable and covers a wide range of possibilities, as indicated in Figure 3.1. Again, the professional evaluation community is a part of this mix.

When internal or external evaluators encounter an ethical dilemma, the context in which they understand and then resolve the dilemma is, therefore,

## Figure 3.1.  A Comparison of Communities for
## Internal and External Evaluators

**Communities for Internal Evaluators**

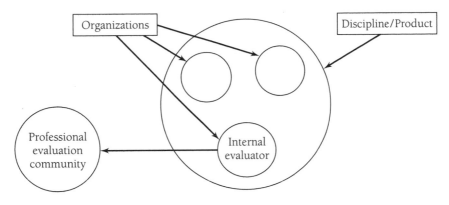

**Communities for External Evaluators**

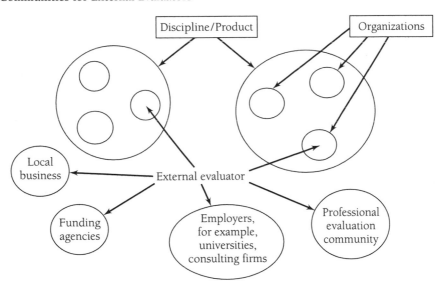

different. I return to the situation I described in the previous section—the demand by my boss or client that I assess student outcomes as part of the evaluation of teacher development projects—to illustrate these differences. As suggested, the occurrence of the dilemma is not related to the internal-external distinction, but I believe the resolution of the dilemma and the impact of that resolution does depend on it.

As an internal evaluator responsible for the evaluation of a teacher development project directed to primary grade teachers and intending to enhance their knowledge and skills in teaching mathematics, I was "enjoined" to assess students' mathematics performance as a part of the evaluation. Given the nature of the intervention and the teachers' serious lack of content and pedagogical knowledge of mathematics, such indicators would likely suggest program failure, whereas other indicators (such as changes in teachers' knowledge about math, amount of time spent teaching math, variety of math activities, and so on) were more connected to the program staff's intentions, better matched to program intensity, and hence more appropriate indicators of program success.

As an internal evaluator, one loses some of the aura of the external expert (Adams, 1985); resolving an ethical dilemma thus often requires what I would call an *action proof*. (I will contrast this with an *academic proof* for an external evaluator.) In other words, although the internal evaluator is presumed to have special expertise, it is not mysterious, and recommendations about what and how to do things probably work best if the evaluator can show her recommendation is sound. An action proof is essentially a "show-me" strategy (rather than a reasoning strategy) requiring a context-specific demonstration. In other words, convincing program staff that something is a right or wrong thing to do must be embedded in that particular context and involve a demonstration also embedded within that context.

In the above example, I suggested to program staff that we look at existing student performance data from the year previous to the project beginning and during the first year of the project to determine the usefulness of such data in evaluating the teacher development project. This demonstration of what the use of student outcome data would show in conjunction with the use of indicators more closely coupled with the program's intents—in other words, showing what are good and not-so-good indicators of the program's success—convinced program staff they might potentially draw unnecessary criticism by focusing on student outcomes rather than teacher outcomes in this evaluation.

This strategy was important within the context of this particular evaluation, but also important insofar as internal evaluators must consider the long-term and related consequences of their choices. Within this organization, such a strategy builds an understanding extending beyond the specific project and into a larger discourse about how to think about appropriate indicators of success. This approach also demonstrates what is probably a greater degree of conciliation on the part of internal evaluators—compromise is important in the creation of a community of people who share larger common goals.

As an external evaluator, I have also been enjoined to assess student performance as an indicator of the success of a teacher development project. In one case, a modest (although expensive) intervention to help elementary teachers use their own schoolyards to teach science, the program developers had promised their funding agency that the project would make a positive difference in student outcomes. As with many innovative curricular approaches, the more likely immediate effect of changes in pedagogy and content is diminished student performance, particularly if what one uses are standard school indicators of such performance. Because the program developers had promised the funding agency such a demonstration, there was significant pressure to use standard student outcome measures. Unlike the internal evaluation situation, providing an academic proof was sufficient. This proof relies more on the invocation of authority and expertise vested in me as an expert evaluator (who is being paid substantial amounts of money for good advice) and the use of other examples from the evaluation and research literature. So illustrations of the negative impact of educational innovations on standardized measures of student achievement were compelling, even though they were not specific to this project or even the particular focus of this project, that is, science.

Although an external evaluator could also use an action proof, there is less demand for it and less need for it, as the external evaluator is much less concerned about the consequences for this project and others within the organization—she may or may not be involved and so has less vested interest in creating contexts for specific kinds of discourse. (I have noted elsewhere that this is a potentially serious problem with external evaluation, and suggest a modified role for external evaluators whereby they would have long-term relationships with organizations, rather than being evaluators of specific activities or projects [Mathison, 1994].) Similarly, although external evaluators want to maintain positive relationships with their clients, they can afford to be less conciliatory than the internal evaluator, as their connections to the organization are circumscribed and particular. And they are afforded more latitude as an expert than is the internal evaluator.

The fundamental basis of these differences is based on the nature of the community to which internal and external evaluators belong. The community for internal evaluators is their workplace; regardless of the kind of organization, they are committed to making that community work well, both in particular instances and in the long term. Their decisions about how to respond to the myriad ethical dilemmas posed by evaluation are contextualized by this primary affiliation with their particular workplace. External evaluators, however, operate in less particularized communities and perhaps the greater unifying community may be that of other evaluators (although I am not suggesting that internal evaluators are not also connected to the community of professional evaluators). Their decisions about how to respond to ethical dilemmas are informed by general practices, other evaluation experience, demands of other work communities, and with reference to what other professional evaluators would do in this sort of instance.

It might be argued that internal evaluators, through their use of action proofs and familiarity with the organization, the program, and the stakeholders, have greater potential for a sustained impact on the ways in which evaluation can contribute to positive outcomes within an organization. (External evaluators might also consider using action proofs as well, even though often an academic proof is sufficient. This might be particularly helpful if an external evaluator adopts principles that support sustained organizational learning and change.) I will argue in the next section that internal evaluators may be less well situated to raise questions about the ethics of the evaluand itself than are external evaluators.

## Judging the Ethics of the Evaluand

The previous section discussed ethical issues related to doing an evaluation well and how the internal-external distinction makes a difference. Evaluators are also meant to judge the ethics of the evaluand—to raise questions about whether the job is being done right and to raise questions about whether the right job is being done, what Hendricks (1985) described as a need to judge the appropriateness of services.

Let me return to my experiences as an internal evaluator for the mathematics project described earlier. This project (actually many projects) adopted an underlying principle that the way to improve schools was to employ a standard research, development, and diffusion model. This model focuses on developing packaged curricular materials and teacher education that can be widely disseminated regardless of the circumstances in which it is implemented. The lack of success of this model is well documented (House, 1981; Mathison, 1990). As the internal evaluator, this approach to educational change seemed to me misguided (given its demonstrated lack of success), equivalent to not doing the right thing. The project might be more successful at real, sustained educational change if it focused on specific schools, working from a grassroots action research model, rather than an expertise-driven research model. As an internal evaluator, it was difficult to raise questions about these fundamental principles within the projects. My expertise was presumed to be in evaluation, understood as expertise in technique, so my reflections on curricular and pedagogical foundations were considered to be less informed than reflections on data analysis strategies, for example. Little that I did was a compelling challenge to the conceptualization of the project, never mind effective in altering these foundational principles.

This is an innocuous example when compared to, for example, addressing issues such as racism, sexism, or classism that may be inherent in a particular program or project. Here, the internal evaluator is often in a weak position to confront these matters, especially if they are rampant within or condoned by the organization. Fear of loss of one's job, friendships, or dissolution of one's community or organization are serious risks for the internal evaluator. The internal evaluator as whistle-blower entails substantial personal and organizational risks. And raising questions about the ethical stance of a project or activity within the organization potentially puts the internal evaluator in a position of questioning her own complicity with unethical practices. External evaluators, while experiencing the above constraints to a certain degree, are in a better position to voice serious concerns, in large part because they do not belong to these organizational or workplace communities and do not need to sustain relationships and commitments to doing a good thing within that context.

For example, as an external evaluator working with a group of doctoral students to evaluate an after-school program for inner-city teens, it was much easier for us to raise issues of racism that were subtle and insidious within the program. The program focused on a transition-to-work idea and, as such, the teens were responsible for finding their own internships within the organizations, in this case a museum. This organization provided a vast array of potentially valuable experiences for them, but for the most part they either floundered about looking for work or worked in menial jobs, such as cleaning in the cafeteria. Underlying the program's inability to provide positive, meaningful work experiences for these teens was a deficit model of inner-city, African-American teens—one that presumed they weren't very able, by definition had psychological problems, and couldn't really be counted on in things that matter. The program itself was ethically flawed. As external evaluators we could much more easily raise these issues of racism than could an internal evaluator. We were not seen as having a vested interest (although the staff did feel betrayed by us for raising these issues, and the teens were grateful for being given an opportunity to reveal their perceptions) and were presumed by our expertise to be doing a fair job. Did the racism diminish as a consequence of the evaluation? I do not think so, but the issue at least got talked about by a range of program stakeholders. This is always the downside for external evaluators—they have the power and authority to raise such issues but little efficacy when it comes to ameliorating unethical programs. Naming unethical programs or practices does not, of course, guarantee their elimination.

Both internal and external evaluators should look at the ethics of the things they evaluate, and I presume they do. Internal evaluators are more at risk when raising such questions than are external evaluators, however.

## Conclusion

Internal and external evaluators experience the same ethical dilemmas and both work toward resolving them in principled, justified ways. However, they occupy different communities, and these communities have an impact on how ethical dilemmas are addressed and what strategies are most effective in resolving them. In some situations internal evaluators have the edge (such as in creating communities of discourse about how to do evaluation well), whereas in other situations external evaluators do (such as in raising questions about unethical intentions or practices within programs). The purpose of this chapter is not to value one situation over the other but to suggest to both internal and external evaluators that thinking about themselves as embedded within communities is one way to proceed in dealing with ethical dilemmas in their practice. Also, the analysis presented here is not meant to suggest that these community structures are fatal in determining how internal and external evaluators might approach ethical dilemmas, and indeed both groups have much to learn from each other.

## References

Adams, K. A. "Gamesmanship for internal evaluators: Knowing when to 'hold 'em' and when to 'fold 'em.'" *Evaluation and Program Planning*, 1985, 8, 53–57.

Dewey, J. *Democracy and Education.* New York: The Free Press, 1916.

Etzioni, A. *The New Golden Rule: Community and Morality in a Democratic Society.* New York: Basic Books, 1996.

Hendricks, M. "Should Evaluators Judge Whether Services Are Appropriate?" *Evaluation and Program Planning*, 1985, 8, 34–44.

House, E. R. "Three Perspectives on Innovation: Technological, Political, and Cultural." In R. Lehming and M. Kane (eds.), *Improving Schools.* Beverly Hills, Calif.: Sage, 1981.

House, E. R. "In-House Reflection: Internal Evaluation." *Evaluation Practice,* 1986, 7 (1), 63–64.

Kirkhart, K. "Analyzing Mental Health Evaluation: Moral and Ethical Dimensions." *Evaluation and Program Planning,* 1985, 8, 13–23.

Love, A. J. (ed.). *Developing Effective Internal Evaluation.* New Directions for Program Evaluation, no. 20. San Francisco: Jossey-Bass, 1983.

Mathison, S. "Reflections on Evaluating Innovative Curriculum Projects." In I. Wirsaup and R. Streit (eds.), *Developments in School Mathematics Education Around the World, Vol. 2.* Reston, Va.: National Council of Teachers of Mathematics, 1990.

Mathison, S. "What Do We Know about Internal Evaluation?" *Evaluation and Program Planning,* 1991a, 14, 159–165.

Mathison, S. "Role Conflicts for Internal Evaluators." *Evaluation and Program Planning,* 1991b, 14, 173–179.

Mathison, S. "Rethinking the Evaluator Role: Partnerships Between Organizations and Evaluators." *Evaluation and Program Planning,* 1994, 17, 299–304.

Morris, M., and Cohn, R. "Program evaluators and ethical challenges: A national survey." *Evaluation Review,* 1993, 17, 621–642.

Patton, M. Q. *Utilization-Focused Evaluation: The New Century Text* (3rd ed). Thousand Oaks, Calif.: Sage, 1997.

Reavy, P., Littel, L., Gonda, G., and O'Neill, I. "Evaluation as Management Support: The Role of the Evaluator." *Canadian Journal of Program Evaluation,* 1993, 8 (2), 95–104.

Scriven, M. "Evaluation Ideologies." In G. F. Maddaus, M. Scriven, and D. L. Stufflebeam (eds.), *Evaluation Models.* Boston: Koewer-Nijoff, 1983.

Smith, N. L. "Some Characteristics of Moral Problems in Evaluation Practice." *Evaluation and Program Planning,* 1985, 8, 5–11.

Winberg, A. "Maximizing the Contribution of Internal Evaluation Units." *Evaluation and Program Planning,* 1991, 14, 167–172.

Worthen, B., Sanders, J., and Fitzpatrick, J. *Program Evaluation: Alternative Approaches and Practical Guidelines.* New York: Longman, 1997.

*SANDRA MATHISON is associate professor in the Department of Educational Theory and Practice at the University at Albany, State University of New York.*

*Foundation staff share their perspectives, as managers and practitioners, on the ethical challenges and opportunities facing professionals engaged in the evaluation of comprehensive, community-based initiatives and other nontraditional program strategies.*

# Ethical Challenges in Evaluation with Communities: A Manager's Perspective

*David Nee, Maria I. Mojica*

We are senior staff members at a family foundation (the W. C. Graustein Memorial Fund) in Connecticut that views evaluation as both a key management tool and an instrument of learning for foundation staff, trustees, grantee organizations, and communities.

Most foundations ground their mission in one or all three traditions of philanthropy—philanthropy as relief, as improvement, and as social reform. In each of these domains, foundations want to know how effective they have been, and what they can do to improve their grant-making. These ambitions as a field, and the day-to-day requirement to know "what works" as managers of philanthropic resources, make us enthusiastic consumers of evaluations. We look to the process and results of evaluations as essential tools. Foundations have become more interested in using evaluation, not just as a "monitoring" or "measuring tool," but as a catalyst that encourages us to be reflective about our grant-making practices and future directions.

## A Shifting Paradigm?

Our background and experience lend perspective to our observations and beliefs about the current and future conduct of evaluations, as well as the ethical issues that arise from this work for the evaluation professional and the sponsoring foundation. Our foundation has budgeted $600,000 for the evaluation of a major multisite initiative designed to improve life and educational outcomes for young children. We are also planning to evaluate an intermediary organization created by the foundation, the Connecticut Center for School Change, that we estimate will cost close to 10 percent of the

Center's operating budget each year. We therefore see ourselves in several related roles: clients of evaluation in the transactional sense; investors, because the Memorial Fund places great credence in evaluation and its ability to build capacity; and, finally, as co-managers, with the evaluator, of a learning process. We seek a partnership among evaluators, communities of interest, technical assistance providers, and the foundation.

Partnership may seem a large claim. We nonetheless believe it to be an appropriate goal and perhaps reflective of a shift in how private grant-making foundations look at evaluation. We see this as part of a larger trend toward more collaborative grant-making, often exemplified in large comprehensive community initiatives. Such efforts include, for instance, the National Funding Collaborative on Violence Prevention and the National Community AIDS Partnership, both funded by many national and local foundations. There are numerous other major initiatives funded by the Pew Charitable Trust, Ford, Annie E. Casey, Mott, Macarthur, and other foundations. There are also equally comprehensive initiatives taking place at the local level. The ten-year commitment to Children and Youth by the Hartford Foundation for Public Giving and a like effort by the Chicago Community Trust are noteworthy for their scale.

According to the Aspen Institute (Roundtable on Comprehensive Community Initiatives for Children and Families, 1997), a comprehensive community initiative is defined as a neighborhood-based effort that has as its goals the improvement of life circumstances for children, families, and other residents. Though these initiatives vary in purpose and scope, many share common characteristics. These initiatives usually embrace programmatic interventions and collaborative strategies designed to increase community capacity, and require high levels of community engagement in initiative design and decision making. This also means high levels of engagement with aspects related to the planning and conduct of the evaluation.

As Carol Weiss (Horsch, 1998) teaches us, the evaluation of such initiatives is extremely difficult and calls for new approaches. These approaches are likely to alter relationships between evaluators and stakeholders, including the foundation sponsor. Large, long-term, multisite initiatives may require more discussion by foundations and evaluators of what constitutes ethical practice. Even if the American Evaluation Association's (AEA) *Guiding Principles for Evaluators* remain the same, the dynamics change when so many actors in the drama are given speaking roles. In particular, many foundations are approaching the community on a new footing. Increasingly, they are trying to respect the community as a full partner with a legitimate voice in shaping evaluation and other program decisions.

We recognize that these shifts may not be as dramatic or far advanced as our enthusiasm. To be sure, evaluation has rarely supplied everything that the consumers have desired from it. As Deborah Prothrow-Stith, assistant dean of the Harvard School of Health, has stated, "We often hear about the weakness of interventions, but rarely hear about the weakness of evaluation methodologies. Yet practitioners have been sure they were having an influence on the lives of young people that program-level evaluations have not been able to measure" (personal communication, 1994). Given that Prothrow-Stith was referring to the field of violence prevention, we might also note that rates of homicide and other assault crimes in many U.S. cities have fallen in recent years, beyond what could apparently be explained by demographics or "get-tough" justice policies. Something happened, but we did not find it in evaluation.

## Our Approach

These new initiatives, the desire to evaluate them, and the struggle to find methods and language sufficient to do so may change the posture of the evaluator. In the course of developing this paper, we did a brief review of relevant articles, a review of the *Guiding Principles for Evaluators*, and a series of lengthy interviews with six colleagues: a manager of a national multisite initiative with multiple evaluation components; an evaluator affiliated with an academic center in a major university; another evaluator who operates a small consulting firm; the head of a large evaluation consulting firm; a senior manager in a large national foundation known for multisite initiatives that seek to enhance community capacity; and the executive of a national foundation known for research and evaluation that is often innovative in substance or method.

We asked each colleague several questions: (1) how they described their experience as evaluation practitioners or managers; (2) how they saw the field of evaluation evolving, and whether they perceived a shift away from third-party, "at-a-distance" work to more consultative, negotiated processes with the people or organizations affected by evaluation; (3) what the typical ethical tensions were in the third-party or consultative role that they considered critical, and whether these tensions differed from those encountered in more consultative relationships; (4) what a foundation's role in evaluation is, especially whether the foundation has special responsibilities toward communities in which it is funding complex interventions; and (5) whether there were other issues, concepts, or questions that ought to arise that we had not addressed. (A definitional note: We are speaking of foundations as entities that primarily make grants to others to provide services or conduct research. We are not talking about grant-seeking institutions that sometimes also call themselves "foundations.")

## What We Found

On the basis of the information we received and our own observations, we believe there are significant and dynamic changes within the field as it relates to evaluation and accountability issues, notably for comprehensive community initiatives. Grant-makers do seem to be seeking a new relationship to the communities they serve that is more of a partnership. Increasingly, foundations appear to seek community input into the very scope and design of evaluations as well as feedback through interim and final reports. Even in the most earnest of such efforts, however, there are inherent inequalities in the power relationship. The foundation, after all, has the resources that the community or organization of interest wants. The foundation is a buyer, with all the power that implies.

In our interviews, we explored whether these new initiatives, relationships, and the efforts to evaluate them are resulting in a new paradigm, one in which the evaluator can be as much participant as observer. We probed whether the evaluator can be regarded, at least in these larger efforts, as totally at arm's length from the intervention itself. Moreover we asked whether this phenomenon grows from the trend toward comprehensive community initiatives.

In the mind of the evaluators we interviewed, this change falls well short of a paradigm shift. Evaluators were quick to point out that there has always been a methodological continuum in the evaluation field from process to outcomes, and that in their view "big science" (meaning rigorous experimental designs with large populations) still happens and still adds the most knowledge. Two of our respondents commented spontaneously on the efficacy of the welfare reform demonstrations carried out by the Manpower Demonstration Research Corporation and others.

Nonetheless, the evaluators did acknowledge that something is shifting, at least in what the market for evaluation seems to demand. Here the foundation managers concur. One evaluator spoke of a greater interest and willingness to get into "intellectually messier" areas. She saw that foundations were placing a higher value on learning over evaluation per se, often with the goal of increasing community capacity. Although the methodological repertoire may remain unchanged, foundations increasingly seek the more consultative forms of evaluation. One foundation executive remarked that sometimes we need the numbers, other times the story. She pointed out how ethnography has deepened our understanding of how children actually grow up in families, and how one researcher used focus groups of family caregivers to enrich standards for day care provided by kin.

One evaluator perceives that these are substantial changes in the marketplace and are accompanied by changes in evaluation: "more professional, more pervasive." The same person notes that the increasing popularity of evaluation based on logic models and theories of change carries the evaluator into a planning arena that might in the past have been addressed by program staff. The evaluator finds that university-based evaluators now compete with private firms to undertake implementation studies that would not have been considered of academic interest in the past; she attributes this change to marketplace dynamics.

One program manager sees the evaluation field in turmoil, challenged to cross an economic, cultural, and educational divide to connect more effectively with communities. She noted that communities of color in particular are extremely skeptical of past evaluation practice.

Finally, a foundation manager notes that his organization considers evaluation as part of the change process, not outside of it. He feels this view calls on the evaluator "to be one of the partners and respect the particularities of time and place."

We are comfortable calling these changes a market shift rather than a paradigm shift, though one individual felt strongly that this is a true difference, not a case of degree. Either way, all perceived increased demand for more consultative process, with more feedback to the foundation and its partners as implementation is unfolding, and concurred that although this consultation does introduce ethical tensions, the tensions can be anticipated. As all of our informants agreed, when you are the third party and at a distance from transactions, you are more easily insulated from ethical tension. When the evaluator is a partner at the table, certain tensions come to the forefront.

## Roles Within a Changing Evaluation Environment

As we have indicated, one effect of such initiatives is to alter the roles of the foundation and the evaluator vis-à-vis the community. At its heart, private grant-making takes us both, foundation staff and evaluator, into an ethically tricky world. Foundations are relatively wealthy compared to the communities they attempt to serve. Despite good intentions, the flow of dollars can potentially lead to the systemic disempowerment of the very communities that the foundation is trying to help. The evaluator also plays a role in this power equation, because information is power, too. If a foundation is serious about providing experiences and resources that allow communities to empower themselves, that foundation must examine all of its practices in light of this tendency toward disempowerment. Re-thinking evaluation is a necessary part of this examination. Other things being equal, people with resources generally do not give enough consideration to the realities and opinions of people without resources. This surfaces in numerous ways that foundation managers are learning to recognize and to use to alter their own behaviors and practices. Evaluation can be an effective mechanism for such reflective practices and for keeping the discussion with the community honest.

Just as communities can experience the interventions of foundations as off the mark or even invasive, so too evaluation may leave communities feeling violated. An outside entity got what it wanted: data and interviews. The community may feel it was left with no substantive legacy. Often the community feels that it has been judged, rather than the intervention, and found wanting. In rigorous designs the evaluator may feel constrained to withhold potentially valuable information to protect the intervention from "contamination." Can evaluator and sponsor enter a new covenant with those being evaluated, without violating professional principles and ethics? Can we provide timely feedback without compromising objectivity? The challenge is how to straddle the proverbial fence without splitting our pants.

Whether the people we talked to believed this change was merely market demand or truly a paradigm shift, they all saw substantial ethical concerns being raised by this more consultative role. Of course, several pointed out that the traditional "at-a-distance" approach to evaluation generates its own, often unacknowledged, ethical strains. As one respondent observed, "You see the program derailing and don't go in and help. You are a bystander." The same person noted that often program managers spend time correcting initial diagnoses by evaluators that are not sufficiently informed.

We are beginning to hear a new language of evaluation in the foundation world, and to observe new practices. We have even tried a few ourselves. Marie Wilson of the Ms. Foundation for Women speaks of a "learning component" rather than evaluation. We believe that more foundations will wish to engage with the community in a mutual process of discovery or learning. Such language and practice are more appropriate to community work than the connotation of judgment that evaluation has in the past often carried.

Many of the ethical challenges associated with this emerging framework are directly or indirectly related to role conflict, that is, "roles or relationships [evaluators] have that might pose a significant conflict of interest with their role as an evaluator" (American Evaluation Association, 1995, p. 23).

All our informants agreed that the consultative role carries more ambiguity and more tension. As one respondent noted, "when the success of the evaluation is equated with program success, life gets tricky." Moreover, an evaluator who is trying to "bias the program for success" in the role of a consultant must not become a cheerleader. Direct feedback is valued: "The real value for me as a practitioner is [hearing] an opinion I do not hold." Otherwise, "the honesty and integrity of the entire evaluation process" (American Evaluation Association, 1995, p. 23) is compromised.

Of course, when there are discrepancies in perspective between the program operator and the evaluator, sponsoring foundations face a problem. Should they assume the credibility of the program operator because he or she may have more intimate knowledge of the intervention or communities involved? Or should they assume that the evaluator is more credible, due to presumed objectivity? Regardless of the foundation's response to this situation, evaluators need to remember that their job is not to make sponsors or operators comfortable, but to abide by the guiding principle of integrity/honesty.

Multisite "comprehensive" initiatives are inherently complex and evolutionary. They may start out using one set of program interventions and change to a different set of interventions as local conditions evolve or opportunities present themselves. Although these changes do not necessarily alter the nature of questions evaluators should ask at the threshold, it does deepen them. Moreover, the developmental nature of the work of comprehensive initiatives often results in the evaluator being asked to assume a technical assistant role. If evaluators accept this role, they become part of the intervention. Although "evaluators must strive to meet legitimate client needs whenever it is feasible and appropriate to do so" (American Evaluation Association, 1995, p. 25), serving as a technical assistant gives the evaluator a vested interest in program success that can interfere with impartial assessment. This ethical challenge can be managed, in part, by carefully documenting the role of the evaluator as a key component of the intervention.

## Ethical Concerns and Solutions

Classically, the sponsor of evaluation, whether government or private foundation, wants data that are at least valid in a policy arena. Conversely, the sponsor also wants to minimize the funds spent on evaluation. There can even be pressure from other stakeholders to reduce the dollars allocated to evaluation in favor of program operations. The evaluator always has an ethical responsibility to provide full disclosure of methods, cost, and potential to yield valid findings. This disclosure becomes even more important in comprehensive community initiatives. Nothing distresses the sponsors of community collaboration more than learning that dollars have been spent on an elaborate evaluation that is not returning knowledge helpful to the future work of the initiative. Moreover, the early discussion of resources and materials can lead to bursts of clarity not merely about the limits of evaluation, but even the shape of the intervention itself. In one case, a large national collaborative wanted to demonstrate the impact of its regranting program through community foundations. After careful investigative work by the evaluator, board members, and others involved in the initiative, the group realized that the five million dollars for a true impact study simply could not be raised. The experience made clear the role for that collaborative as chiefly a mechanism for raising and distributing funds to local partners, not as a major generator of new knowledge in the first instance. Carol Weiss of the Harvard School of Education speaks to this directly: "Evaluation takes time, resources, and skill. Evaluators should not take on studies when they know they cannot do a good job. . . . They can argue back, explain that the time is too short, the requisite data are unavailable, appropriate comparisons are missing, the money is insufficient for the size of the task or whatever the problems may be. It is not easy to do" (Horsch, 1998, pp. 5–6).

Many evaluators will quickly say, "But we are always required to do this." True. As Guiding Principle C.1 indicates, "Evaluators should negotiate honestly with clients and relevant stakeholders concerning the costs, tasks to be undertaken, limitations of methodology, scope of results likely to be obtained, and uses of data resulting from a specific evaluation" (American Evaluation Association, 1995, p. 23). We simply note that the characteristics of comprehensive community initiatives set up higher levels of ethical tension because the ambitions of sponsors tend to rise proportionately to their financial investment and their proximity to the work. Therefore, the distance between what the sponsor wants and what the evaluation field can economically supply may be greater than for more traditional program interventions. This dynamic tension can also produce creative thinking about the methodology. Methods may be found to supply 80 percent of what is sought at 20 percent of the effort. Depending on the foundation's goals and the decision-making arena, that can be good enough. Nonetheless, we believe these complexities make a case in which the differences in degree may add up to a difference in kind. Therefore, if the current interest in comprehensive community initiatives continues among foundation directors and managers, evaluators will be asked to think and behave differently. The need for innovative methodologies will increase, and as they are developed, the standards of competence that evaluators must meet in order for them to engage in ethical practice will increase as well.

Our informants emphasized "cross-boundary" communications as one of the keys to managing ethical tensions when working within the community. There must be early and continuing discussion among foundation managers, technical assistance providers, evaluators, program managers, and community. One evaluator cautions that this "communication should not happen in dyads." The communication itself may be tense. The people who have the most frequent contact with community—regardless of role—may begin to behave as advocates for the community with the other partners. Dyadic conversations may exacerbate such tensions, whereas broader group discussion can provide a self-connecting mechanism. Moreover, dyads may put the foundation as power-broker at the center; group conversations at least allow for consensus to develop and help keep the focus on the intervention.

Both the sponsors of evaluation and the evaluator must be resolute in seeking clarity about mutual expectations, must revisit them frequently, and must be explicit about the ethical dimensions of the expectations. We say "frequently" especially in the case of multisite efforts promoting community change because the interventions may merely be sketched at the outset and in all likelihood may shift appropriately during the life of the initiative. Such changes have obvious consequences for the allocation of evaluation and technical assistance resources. Anticipating change and rehearsing the process for making such alterations is preferable to trying to figure out a process in the middle of a crisis.

These discussions should begin with a frank statement of the purpose of the evaluation. Is the evaluation being done to build knowledge in the field, or to build the capacity of the site? For accountability to the foundation's board? For publicity and fundraising? Each purpose presupposes different tasks, approaches, and perhaps different people on teams. For instance, if the real purpose is fundraising, perhaps good documentation is enough and a journalist with oversight from an evaluator could do the job. If the job is capacity-building, questions about coordinating evaluation with technical assistance immediately arise, among a host of other complications. If the purpose emphasizes accountability and summative decisions, different relations are needed.

The foundation and the evaluator should strive for clarity about purpose, implications of that purpose for other parties, truth telling about what the evaluation requires (not only financial resources, but human resources, and calls on the time and effort of communities, program staff, and technical assistance providers), avoidance of premature and false precision (you can't start with outcomes before the intervention is specified and deeply understood), and a strategy for continuing communications among involved parties.

The changing environment has resulted in evaluators serving much more frequently as teachers, consultants, and technical assistants. We in the foundation world speak of attempting "to bias the intervention for success." Rather than withholding data for a summative judgment at the end of a long period of intervention, the evaluator supplies data and observations as the initiative unfolds, with a view toward restructuring the initiative to be more effective. This instantly makes the evaluator a consultant to both foundation and community and in the odd position—from an ethical point of view—of assessing the efficacy of his or her own advice. The evaluator has become a partner in the success or failure of the enterprise and yet is still expected to report candidly on the success of the intervention. Are these dual, potentially conflicting, roles appropriate?

Furthermore, few comprehensive multisite initiatives operate only through a foundation staff and evaluators. More often, the foundation has a separate technical assistance function to support the community initiatives as well. Yet we also expect the evaluator to deliver technical assistance. This raises two issues: One is the technical issue of deciding what kind of assistance is to be provided by the evaluator, and settling on a communication mechanism among the technical assistance broker, the evaluator, and the foundation staff. The other issue is ethical: The evaluator again is put in the position of influencing the intervention to be evaluated. The evaluator's influence always has the potential to affect the outcome of the intervention anyway. Here the influence is more explicit and, therefore, can be more clearly identified and taken into consideration as a factor.

Absorbing all of this, we suggest some areas of questions that evaluators may wish to address if they are invited to the community collaboration table by a sponsoring foundation:

1. If the foundation wishes to make big claims about partnering with the community, what is the extent of the foundation's involvement with it? Have plans in development been discussed with the community? What was the nature of these discussions? Has the foundation conducted focus groups with community residents, shared draft plans, or convened representative advisory groups?

2. What are the foundation's expectations about the evaluator's role beyond describing the initiative or assessing its impact? Does the foundation anticipate a technical assistance role? In what form? How broad? Does the foundation also expect to deliver technical assistance from other sources? If so, how does all this work get orchestrated?

3. If the foundation expects the evaluator to help provide information to "bias for success," what are the important landmarks of internal decision making? What information will the foundation seek to have available at that time? What kind of separation is appropriate between the evaluator's observations and the foundation's decisions?

4. How will evaluators and foundations address the ethical strain if the intervention proves to be persistently weak and the evaluators have been involved in recommending changes? Will committing to a dissemination plan before the results are known prevent suppressed reports later?

5. Do the resources allocated by the foundation fit the job? Are the questions truly answerable? To undertake an under-resourced evaluation or gloss over methodological difficulties is always a problem within the ethics of evaluation. Complex comprehensive community initiative make this issue even more relevant.

## Closing Note

In this era there is growing interest in improving the capacity of communities, whether one calls it "asset-based" grant-making, restoring civil society, enhancing social capital, or simply doing good civic work. Evaluators play a paradoxically larger and more elastic role in the complex initiatives designed to enhance community capacity, often by teaching communities themselves how to generate and use data strategically. The advice we have garnered about ethics in this environment comes down to these points for both evaluators and their sponsors:

1. Do no harm. Evaluation is to help and enlighten, not to distract or further disorganize stressed communities.
2. Respect differences. The evaluator must be able to negotiate and communicate with diverse populations and constituencies and to hear and learn their histories and concerns.
3. Keep the evaluation from taking on such a life of its own that it distracts program and community "from the simmering cauldron of the change process itself," as one of our informants put it. Design elegantly to minimize the distraction.
4. Think about legacy from the opening moment of design. What will be left behind for the community? Evaluators and sponsors have an obligation to leave something behind—for instance, a community capacity for the strategic development and use of data, or a set of community spokespeople who can talk knowledgeably about the intervention, its outcomes, and their evaluation.
5. Carry an awareness that if the intellectual ownership of the intervention remains with the sponsor and evaluator, not much may change. If the community has been recruited into evaluative work, however, there is the potential of an internalized change process that can go forward well after the evaluator and foundation have departed from the scene.
6. Finally, remember that the evaluator has a fundamental role, as one of our informants stated, "to incite reflection."

If evaluation is truly becoming a learning component, and the community becomes the classroom, the evaluator becomes the chief facilitator of learning experiences for the other partners.

## References

American Evaluation Association, Task Force on Guiding Principles for Evaluators. "Guiding Principles for Evaluators." In W. R. Shadish, D. L. Newman, M. A. Scheirer, and C. Wye (Eds.), *Guiding Principles for Evaluators.* New Directions for Program Evaluation, No. 66. San Francisco: Jossey-Bass, 1995.

Horsch, K. "Interview with Carol H. Weiss." *The Evaluation Exchange: Emerging Strategies in Evaluating Child and Family Services,* 1998, *4,* 5–6.

Roundtable on Comprehensive Community Initiatives for Children and Families. *Voices from the Field: Learning from the Early Work of Comprehensive Community Initiatives.* Washington, D.C.: Aspen Institute, 1997.

*DAVID NEE is executive director at the William Caspar Graustein Memorial Fund. The Memorial Fund is a private family foundation in Connecticut. The foundation works statewide to improve education outcomes and foster personal growth and leadership.*

*MARIA I. MOJICA is senior program officer at the William Caspar Graustein Memorial Fund.*

*This chapter focuses on ethical issues that can arise in the collection
and analysis of data in evaluations. We move beyond common ethical
issues in data collection and analysis, such as informed consent and
coercion, to address four issues: the application of cost-benefit thinking
to judgments about research ethics, the quality of research design as an
ethical issue, the need to explore one's data, and the censoring of data.*

# The Ethics of Data Collection
and Analysis

*Melvin M. Mark, Kristen M. Eyssell, Bernadette Campbell*

Data collection and analysis have been an important focus in discussions of
ethics in evaluation almost since the beginning of a separately identifiable literature on evaluation. Issues related to data collection and analysis are at the
heart of the Evaluation Research Society's *Standards for Program Evaluation*
(Rossi, 1982). Such issues are featured prominently, amid a broader set of concerns, in both the American Evaluation Association's (AEA) *Guiding Principles
for Evaluators* (American Evaluation Association, 1995) and the Joint Committee's (1994) *Program Evaluation Standards*. Issues related to data collection
and analysis also arise in practice-based case discussions of ethics in evaluation (for example, Esbensen and others, 1996; Gensheimer, Ayers, and Roosa,
1993; Johnson, 1985). This attention to data collection and analysis in the literature on ethics in evaluation is not surprising: Data collection and analysis,
whether qualitative, quantitative, or both, is a central part of the practice of
evaluation. Indeed, the first of AEA's Guiding Principles is that "Evaluators conduct systematic, data-based inquiries about whatever is being evaluated"
(American Evaluation Association, 1995).

In this chapter, we briefly summarize several of the long-standing ethical issues that arise with respect to data collection and analysis, such as
informed consent and confidentiality. In this context, we discuss and raise
questions about the cost-benefit framework that is often applied to decisions about the ethics of data collection and analysis. We then address three
issues that are less commonly discussed in the context of ethics but have
been identified as ethical issues (Rosenthal, 1994): the overall quality of

one's evaluation design, the principled exploration of one's data, and the censoring of data or of findings.

## Classic Issues in Data Collection and Analysis

The usual guidelines about ethics in data collection and analysis can be summarized in a fairly brief form. Risks to participants should be minimized. To the extent that there are risks, the research should take place only if the potential benefits outweigh the risks. Participants should be fully informed about the research, especially potential risks. Deviations from fully informed consent should occur only if the research involves minimal risk and could not reasonably be carried out with fully informed consent. Individuals should be able to choose freely to participate, without coercion. Participants' privacy and decency should be respected. If data cannot be collected anonymously, confidentiality should be preserved to the fullest extent possible. With respect to data collection and analysis, standard ethical guidelines also mandate that one avoid fraud and follow technical requirements. These guidelines are suggested by several codes, including the AEA Guiding Principles and the Joint Committee Standards; in particular, see principle D.1–5 and JCS Propriety Standards 3–4 and Accuracy Standards 1–10.

Of course, as the expression goes, the devil is in the details. The challenge is not in identifying general ethical guidelines, but in making decisions in the context of a particular evaluation. This challenge can be intensified by potential tradeoffs, either between two ethical principles or between an ethical principle and some technical goal. Consider, for example, the ethical guideline that participation should occur freely and without coercion. Coercion is easy to identify in some cases, as when prisoners are ordered to participate, but may not be so clear in other cases. In particular, at some point inducements to participate, including cash payments for completing questionnaires, can cross the line into coercion (Mariner, 1990). But where is the line between acceptable inducement and unacceptable coercion? Moreover, inducements may contribute to a high response rate, and this desirable technical attribute may sometimes be important for key evaluation users. Could large inducements simultaneously put clients at risk of coercion *and* increase the acceptability of this and other risks by increasing the expected benefits of an evaluation? The devil is indeed in the details.

## Cost-Benefit Analysis of Research as an Ethical Guideline

A form of cost-benefit analysis is often recommended to researchers trying to exorcize the devil from the details. According to this viewpoint, the risks to participants are to be weighed against the potential benefits of the research. This approach is advocated in many of the ethical codes to which evaluators and others look, including the *Code of Federal Regulations,* which provides the guidelines on which most institutional review boards are based (U.S. Department of Health and Human Services, 1998), and the ethical guidelines of many major professional associations (see, for example, American Psychological Association, 1992). The AEA Guiding Principles also make reference to the weighing of costs and benefits (D.1 and 2).

Despite the widespread acceptance of the cost-benefit framework, it can be challenging to implement in practice. Neither the risks nor the benefits of an evaluation (or other inquiry) can be perfectly known in advance. For instance, in evaluating a program for families involved in family court, Johnson (1985) acknowledged that he could not predict whether cases would arise that would require confidentiality violations. Estimating benefits and costs is especially difficult when evaluation questions and methods are expected to emerge over the course of the evaluation, as in many participatory evaluations. The estimation of costs and benefits can also be biased by a natural human tendency, whereby evaluators may generally overestimate the benefits and underestimate the risks of their own work.

Another complexity arises because those who bear the costs may not reap the benefits. Benefits can accrue either to participants (as when a program evaluation results in a more effective treatment for current clients), or to others (as when an evaluation leads to a more effective program for later clients, or results in cost savings to society without any gain in program effectiveness). Balancing such benefits is complex, especially if the costs are directly borne by current clients (Mariner, 1990).

Yet another complication arises in evaluation. The evaluand (for example, a social program) itself may have costs and benefits separate from those of the evaluation. Our suggestion is that if the program would be delivered even if there were no evaluation, the costs and benefits of the program should not be included when considering the ethics of evaluation procedures. However, if the services are only delivered in conjunction with the evaluation, as in many demonstration projects, the costs and services of the program should also be considered.

Despite such complications, the cost-benefit framework remains a useful way of thinking about ethical issues in data collection, at least in some conditions. For example, if an evaluation was likely to cause a moderate burden for program clients and personnel, it seems appropriate to consider the expected magnitude of benefits. Though useful as a guide, however, the cost-benefit framework does not mechanically provide answers. It can only serve as an aid to people as they wrestle with an ethical judgment—and it indirectly raises vexing questions, some of which we now address.

## Design Quality and Likelihood of Use as Ethical Issues

Embedded in the cost-benefit approach to research ethics is the notion that there is an ethical dimension to the quality of an evaluation design. Writing about psychological research, Rosenthal (1994) takes the cost-benefit approach to its logical extreme and argues that if a study has a low-quality design relative to its goals, it is unethical. In Rosenthal's (1994) words, "Bad science makes for bad ethics" (p. 128; for a similar statement about evaluation, see Merton, 1990, p. 508). Rosenthal's argument is premised in part on the recognition that studies always have some costs. These include the costs of staff and participant time, the possible costs of inaccurate conclusions based on a poorly designed study, and the opportunity costs of the alternative study or services that otherwise could have been funded. In light of such inevitable costs, Rosenthal argues, design quality is not just a technical issue. If the benefits of a study are zero, then, according to Rosenthal, it should be judged as unethical because it certainly has *some* costs.

Rosenthal's position is not universally accepted. Pomerantz (1994) points out that we can instead describe poorly designed or otherwise flawed studies in terms of their technical shortcomings or inefficiencies. Pomerantz acknowledges that *in principle* one can argue that any squandering of resources is unethical. Nevertheless, Pomerantz contends, it is a disservice to label any and all incompetency or inefficiency as unethical.

Rosenthal's position and Pomerantz's counterargument can be extended, with some additional complexities, to evaluation. The complexities arise because, in evaluation, use can be considered in addition to (or instead of) design quality as an ethical mandate. Consequently, there are a range of positions that evaluators could take. At one extreme, an evaluator could contend, akin to Pomerantz, that design quality and use are not ethical issues. At the other extreme, expanding Rosenthal's position to evaluation, one might argue that bad evaluation design and low likelihood of use both make for bad ethics. Intermediate positions exist that emphasize the importance only of design quality (or of some broader set of factors that determine potential utility; we do not elaborate all the alternatives here). Moreover, these alternative positions can be integrated in a contingent approach to the cost-benefit analyses of evaluation ethics. The key to this contingent approach comes in recognizing that potential risk to participants can be treated as a dimension ranging from no risk to extreme risk, and that ethics may require that different standards be met at different levels of risk.

For studies with low risk, we argue, design quality and likelihood of use should not be viewed primarily from the lens of ethicality. Imagine that participation is not burdensome and that no harm will plausibly come to participants. For example, an evaluation might be based on existing data without personal identifiers, as in many time series studies. If there is a poor design (for example, a strong history effect is not accounted for) or little chance of utilization, criticism of the evaluation should focus on quality or efficiency but not ethics. One might argue that this position is in conflict with the principle concerning competence (B). We, however, see no conflict here. We believe that competence, even in the context of the AEA Guiding Principles, can be viewed as a *professional* rather than an ethical principle.

In many evaluations, there is a modest level of costs and risks to participants. Perhaps the measurement components are somewhat uncomfortable or taxing. When there is a modest level of risk, we argue, high-quality design may offset such costs. If the design is strong, relative to the evaluation's goals, the resulting information gain is sufficient to justify the costs. The notion is that although design quality may not lead simply to direct use, it does contribute greatly to the *potential utility* of an evaluation. For example, in the public sector, good evaluation has worthwhile benefits as an input into democratic institutions and processes, even if evaluation does not directly drive decisions (Mark, Henry, and Julnes, forthcoming). By way of analogy, the free press is not faulted if it fairly and accurately reports a problem but government does not act. Of course, even though design quality may suffice to offset moderate risk, the first priority should be to reduce risk if possible. If risk cannot be reduced without compromising the integrity of the study, then the cost-benefit ratio should be considered (American Psychological Association, 1992).

In some evaluations, the costs and risks for participants are higher. Perhaps the organizational dynamics make it difficult for clients to feel that they are free to refuse to participate in the evaluation, as in evaluations in prisons or in the military. At present, clinical trials of HIV vaccines may epitomize evaluations that hold high risk for participants (Mariner, 1990). When costs and risks are high, we believe a strong case can be made that evaluators need to consider not only design quality, but also the likelihood of use in deciding whether it is ethical to proceed. With the higher risk to participants comes a higher standard for benefits. When risks for participants are high, a utilization focus (Patton, 1997) becomes an ethical mandate, necessary to justify the high risk. However, at some level of extremely high cost, considerations of design quality and utilization become irrelevant. To take an extreme example, no level of expected benefit could justify the atrocities of the Nazi concentration camp experiments or the Tuskegee syphilis study.

This contingent view recognizes, first, that cost-benefit considerations commonly influence our judgments about the ethicality of evaluation procedures, but second, that there are limits to the cost-benefit approach, such that the importance of design quality and likelihood of use for ethical judgments depends on the level of risk. Of course, difficulties can arise in applying the contingent view in practice. Two evaluators may disagree about precisely where the cutoffs are between one standard and another. Or they may disagree about how much risk is associated with a given research procedure or about the level of design quality.

We have sidestepped, to this point, specifying what we mean by design quality. Although we cannot provide a comprehensive explication here of the strengths and weaknesses of all designs—qualitative, quantitative, and mixed—we can at least give a general sense of the term. We use the term design more broadly than the Campbell and Stanley (1966) X and O sense. For us, design quality includes whether the right questions are asked. For example, our broad view of design quality includes decisions about whether to focus on outcomes, implementation processes, costs, and so on. Beyond that, design quality involves whether the evidence that is collected and analyzed provides a reasonable warrant for conclusions about the questions at hand. Stated differently, are the evaluation methods adequate to achieve the evaluation's purpose? How strong is the evidentiary and inferential chain from data to conclusions? Although design quality may be judged by somewhat different criteria in qualitative and quantitative studies, the underlying issues are the same.

Nevertheless, there will be disagreements about the costs and benefits of entire evaluations and of specific procedures within an evaluation. At the end of this chapter, we briefly discuss deliberative procedures to try to resolve such disagreements. First, we discuss an important implication of the cost-benefit approach for data analysis.

## Principled Discovery as an Ethical Consideration

To the extent that benefits are important in assessing research ethics, we argue that it is unethical to fail to explore one's data to learn the lessons they can reveal. For the most part, exploration is not a problem in qualitative research, especially in those traditions that encourage the researcher to iterate between hypothesis generation and hypothesis testing (see Smith, 1997, for an example). However, data exploration runs counter to a powerful tradition in quantitative methods that one should specify predictions *a priori*, test for significance, and then stop so as to maintain the integrity of one's alpha level.

In the context of his cost-benefit analysis of research design, Rosenthal (1994) advocates "data snooping," claiming that "exploitation [of data] is beautiful" (p. 130). Rosenthal contends that given the costs of data collection, it is unethical not to probe one's data fully. But how is one to learn the lessons of one's data, without being misled by some unreplicable, chance pattern? This question may seem unnecessary to those trained in qualitative traditions in which they review the data as a whole, induce assertions, weigh the evidence pro and con, revise the assertions, and continue to iterate between the claims and the evidence, revising claims as needed (Smith, 1997). Quantitative researchers, however, need better models for data exploitation.

Mark, Henry, and Julnes (1998) use the term *principled discovery* to refer to analysis strategies that exploit one's data without being exploitative. There are, in a sense, two aspects to principled discovery: (1) techniques for exploring one's data, and (2) strategies to make the exploration principled and not unabashed snooping. The exploration component, in a quantitative study, can involve a variety of techniques, such as the exploratory use of multiple regression or quantitative techniques to probe possible moderators of treatment effects, or the review of residuals from a regression analyses to guide a search for possible moderators (Mark, Henry, and Julnes, 1998). The disciplining component also can involve a variety of techniques, from statistical adjustments (such as Bonferroni adjustments for multiple comparisons), through reporting techniques (for example, explicit presentation of one's data exploration and its inferential implications), to formal replication.

Julnes (1995) proposed an important means of principled discovery that he calls the *context-confirmatory approach*. In essence, this approach calls for the evaluator, first, to explore the data and seek to learn its lessons. For example, in an evaluation of the Resource Mother Program in which lay home visitors provided support to at-risk pregnant adolescents, Julnes found that the program was effective on average in reducing the rate of low-birth-weight deliveries. In further exploration, Julnes found that the effects were larger for older than for younger mothers. If the initial snooping pays off with an interesting pattern, as in the Resource Mother Program, the next step is to construct an explanation, often by invoking an underlying mechanism. Julnes posited that younger mothers' needs were more tangible and task oriented, and not necessarily met by the Resource Mothers, some of whom placed greater emphasis on providing emotional support than on encouraging proper prenatal care. The final step, which adds principle to the discovery, is to specify a new prediction, derived from the new explanation, and to test it. For instance, Julnes differentiated the support mothers on the basis of the extent to which they provided tangible support versus emotional support. As expected, the program was especially ineffective for younger mothers when the support mothers emphasized emotional support. Principled discovery led to a more beneficial evaluation.

## Censoring as an Ethical Issue

Censoring of data and of findings is an important ethical issue (Rosenthal, 1994). Censoring can occur before data are collected, at the time of analysis, or in reporting. Censoring can be carried out by the evaluator, by the evaluation funder, or by some other stakeholder. For example, funders sometimes censor in advance by restricting evaluators from collecting a prospective outcome variable, or later by restricting either the reporting of a specific finding or the distribution of the findings generally. Evaluators also sometimes censor data or findings, often for technical reasons such as the unavailability of reliable and valid measures of some variable of interest. Whatever the source and timing of the censoring, it can raise important ethical considerations. When censoring takes place for any reason, in general we believe it should be described and explained in evaluation reports (see also GP E.3.; JSC Propriety Standard 6).

We acknowledge that a case can be made for some forms of censoring. For example, evaluation contracts sometimes allow funders the right to control dissemination and publication of evaluation findings. From a utilization-focused perspective, this might facilitate the exploration of issues that would be inhibited by public attention and thereby increase utilization. However, such agreements are probably inappropriate for publicly supported programs, where the public is a critical evaluation audience.

In addition, censoring removes the possibility of one important benefit of evaluation: contributing to subsequent meta-analyses and other forms of synthesis. Rosenthal (1994, p. 130) identifies "meta-analysis as an ethical imperative" because of the potential contribution of meta-analysis. In evaluation, syntheses of findings can allow evaluators to better judge whether and under what conditions programs or policies work. Meta-analyses and other forms of synthesis are also useful for drawing conclusions about generalizability and for developing theories of interventions (Cook, 1993; Lipsey, 1997). The increasing role of evaluation syntheses adds to the ethical cost of censoring: To the extent evaluation reports are censored, syntheses cannot fulfill their promise.

## Deliberative Processes as a Way to Adjudicate Ethical Questions

Even if everyone were to agree on a set of ethical principles, difficulties would occur in applying them in practice. Even if evaluators agree on the contingent view of cost-benefit analysis, they might disagree about how much risk a given procedure entails. Investigators may tend to overestimate the benefits and underestimate the costs of their evaluations. How are such disagreements to be resolved? How are participants to be protected in light of such divergent views?

One perspective that we find compelling is Putnam's (1990) argument that moral issues are not puzzles to be solved through some technical approach, but instead are issues to be adjudicated through some form of social deliberation. Interestingly, contemporary practices about research ethics do include a deliberative social mechanism to adjudicate ethical questions: institutional review boards (IRBs). By having a diverse set of individuals, including community representatives, review proposed research, participants are protected against the perhaps idiosyncratic and egocentric views of individual evaluators.

Moving beyond IRBs, questions of ethics can fruitfully be addressed through a variety of deliberative techniques. Review panels for funding agencies typically consider the ethics of proposed evaluations. Major evaluations often have advisory panels that can be consulted about ethical as well as other issues. Evaluators can engage in formal or informal discussions about questions of ethics. EvalTalk or other electronic networks can serve as a useful forum. In short, it is perhaps better not to dance with the devil alone.

# References

American Evaluation Association, Task Force on Guiding Principles for Evaluators. "Guiding Principles for Evaluators." In W. R. Shadish, D. L. Newman, M. A. Scheirer, and C. Wye (eds.), *Guiding Principles for Evaluators*. New Directions for Program Evaluation, no. 66. San Francisco: Jossey-Bass, 1995.

American Psychological Association. *Ethical Principles in the Conduct of Research with Human Participants*. Washington, D.C.: American Psychological Association, 1992. (Also see APA's Ethical Principles and Code of Conduct at http://www.apa.org/ethics/code.html)

Campbell, D. T., and Stanley, J. C. *Experimental and Quasi-Experimental Designs for Research*. Chicago: Rand McNally, 1966.

Cook, T. D. "A Quasi-Sampling Theory of the Generalization of Causal Relationships" In L. B. Sechrest and A. G. Scott (eds.), *Understanding Causes and Generalizing about Them*. New Directions for Program Evaluation, no. 57. San Francisco: Jossey-Bass, 1993.

Esbensen, F.-A., and others. "Active Parental Consent in School-Based Research: An Examination of Ethical and Methodological Issues." *Evaluation Review*, 1996, *20* (6), 737–753.

Gensheimer, L. K., Ayers, T. S., and Roosa, M. W. "School-Based Prevention Interventions for At-Risk Populations: Practical and Ethical Issues." *Evaluation and Program Planning*, 1993, *16*, 159–167.

Johnson, P. L. "Ethical Dilemmas in Evaluating Programs with Family Court Related Clients." *Evaluation and Program Planning*, 1985, *8*, 45–51.

Joint Committee on Standards for Educational Evaluation. *Standards for Evaluation of Educational Programs, Projects, and Materials*. New York: McGraw-Hill, 1981.

Julnes, G. "Context-confirmatory Methods for Supporting Disciplined Induction in Post-Positivist Inquiry." Paper presented at the Annual Meeting of the American Evaluation Association, Vancouver, British Columbia, November 2, 1995.

Lipsey, M. W. "What Can You Build with Thousands of Bricks? Musings on the Cumulation of Knowledge in Program Evaluation." In D. J. Rog and D. Fournier (Eds.), *Progress and Future Directions in Evaluation: Perspectives on Theory, Practice, and Methods*. New Directions for Evaluation, no. 76. San Francisco: Jossey-Bass, 1997.

Mariner, W. K. "The Ethical Conduct of Clinical Trials of HIV Vaccines." *Evaluation Review*, 1990, *14* (5), 538–564.

Mark, M. M., Henry, G. T., and Julnes, G. "A Realist Theory of Evaluation Practice." In G. T. Henry, G. Julnes, and M. M. Mark (eds.), *Realist Evaluation: An Emerging Theory in Support of Practice*. New Directions for Program Evaluation, no. 78. San Francisco: Jossey-Bass, 1998.

Mark, M. M., Henry, G. T., and Julnes, G. *Evaluation, a Realist Theory: Description, Classification, Causal Analysis, and Values Inquiry*. San Francisco: Jossey Bass, forthcoming.

Merton, V. "Community-based AIDS Research." *Evaluation Review*, 1990, *14* (5), 502–537.

Patton, M. Q. *Utilization-focused Evaluation: The New Century Text*. Thousand Oaks, Calif.: Sage, 1997.

Pomerantz, J. R. "On Criteria for Ethics in Science: Commentary on Rosenthal." *Psychological Science*, 1994, *5* (3), 135–136.

Putnam, H. *Realism with a Human Face*. Cambridge, Mass.: Harvard University Press, 1990.

Rosenthal, R. "Science and Ethics in Conducting, Analyzing, and Reporting Psychological Research." *Psychological Science*, 1994, *5* (3), 127–134.

Rossi, P. H. (Ed.) *Standards for Program Evaluation*. Potomac, Md.: ERS, 1981. New Directions for Program Evaluation, no. 15. San Francisco: Jossey-Bass, 1982.

Smith, M. L. (1997). "Mixing and Matching: Methods and Models." In J. C. Greene and D. J. Caracelli (eds.). *Advances in Mixed-Method Evaluation: The Challenges and Benefits of Integrating Diverse Paradigms*. New Directions for Evaluation, No. 74. San Francisco: Jossey-Bass.

U.S. Department of Health and Human Services. "Protection of Human Subjects." *Code of Federal Regulations*, 1998, *45*, 106–125.

MELVIN M. MARK *is professor of psychology at Pennsylvania State University and editor of the* American Journal of Evaluation. *His publications include the coedited volumes* Social Science and Social Policy, Multiple Methods in Program Evaluation, *and* Realist Evaluation: An Emerging Theory in Support of Practice, *and forthcoming books on a realist theory of evaluation (with Gary Henry and George Julnes) and on quasi-experimentation (with Chip Reichardt).*

KRISTEN M. EYSSELL *is a doctoral candidate in social psychology at Pennsylvania State University. Her research interests include interpersonal relationships, affect regulation, and research methodology.*

BERNADETTE CAMPBELL *is a graduate student in social psychology at Pennsylvania State University. She is currently participating in the evaluation of a prevention program for at-risk youth. In addition to evaluation and prevention research, her interests include the psychology of prejudice and discrimination.*

*The authors review ethical dilemmas in evaluation that emerge from efforts to promote use within a context of stakeholder participation. Case examples illustrate two potentially problematic domains: stakeholder selection and depth of stakeholder involvement. Also discussed are mediating factors in the occurrence and resolution of these dilemmas.*

# Ethical Dimensions of Stakeholder Participation and Evaluation Use

*Rosalie T. Torres, Hallie Preskill*

Ethical issues "which arise in evaluations of social programs . . . are not like legal problems, marked by formal charges and the presumption of innocence until proven guilty. They are more pervasive, often less distinct, and less amenable to confident resolution" (Stake and Mabry, 1997, p. 1). Newman and Brown's (1996) work on applied ethics addresses the complexity and heterogeneity of ethical issues facing program evaluators by describing them in terms of the different roles evaluators fulfill: consultant/administrator, data collector/researcher, reporter, member of a profession, member of society. At any given time during an evaluation, the evaluator is acting in at least two or more of these roles and faces a variety of circumstances in which ethical dilemmas can arise. This chapter focuses on ethical dilemmas stemming from evaluators' efforts to facilitate evaluation use. And although Newman and Brown's reporter role is most closely associated with evaluation use, we are concerned with evaluation use as it applies throughout the evaluation, particularly as use is facilitated through stakeholder participation.

Although stakeholder involvement has long been an expectation of good evaluation practice (see Joint Committee on Standards for Educational Evaluation, 1981), perusal of the evaluation literature over the past ten years quickly reveals that interest in this aspect of evaluation has been increasing (see, for example, Cousins, Donohue, and Bloom, 1996; Cousins and Earl, 1992, 1995; Fetterman, 1994; Greene, 1988; Guba and Lincoln, 1989; House and Howe, 1998; O'Sullivan and O' Sullivan, 1998; Patton, 1997; Preskill and Torres, 1999; Shulha, 1994; Torres, Preskill, and Piontek, 1996). Indeed, a substantial percentage of respondents to a recent survey of members of the American Evaluation Association's (AEA) Topical Interest Group on Evaluation Use

(Preskill and Caracelli, 1997) believes that stakeholder involvement leads to greater use of evaluation findings (74 percent) *and* evaluation processes (72 percent). Stakeholder involvement has the potential to (1) make the evaluation more responsive to various stakeholders' perspectives and information needs, (2) increase the validity of the evaluation when stakeholders engage in dialogue to interpret findings and construct meaning, (3) increase stakeholders' inquiry skills, and (4) help make stakeholders more sophisticated consumers of, and participants in, other evaluation efforts.

In the remainder of this chapter we explore specific areas in which ethical issues related to stakeholder participation and evaluation use can arise and examine case examples for each. The chapter concludes with a discussion of factors mediating the resolution of these issues and suggestions for evaluator practice.

## Ethical Challenges and Issues Related to Stakeholder Participation

How interaction and shared responsibility with stakeholders is negotiated and carried out creates the potential for a variety of ethical dilemmas in program evaluation. In their research on evaluation ethics, Newman and Brown (1996) found frequent or serious violations of evaluation practice related to stakeholder participation, such as (1) evaluators making decisions without consulting with the client, (2) evaluators doing evaluation for their own self-interest, not for the benefit of the client, and (3) evaluators being more respectful toward project management (or a special interest group) than toward staff. These reported violations, based on the experiences of program administrators and staff, do not include information about the extent of stakeholder involvement originally planned or achieved. Our concern is that as wider stakeholder participation is sought in an effort to increase an evaluation's validity, meaningfulness, and use, the potential for at least some types of ethical dilemmas may also increase. The following sections address ethical challenges in two major dimensions of stakeholder participation: which stakeholders to involve, and how to involve them.

**Which Stakeholders Should Be Involved?** Almost all respondents to the aforementioned survey of evaluators (95 percent) agreed that "evaluators should take responsibility for involving stakeholders in the evaluation" (Preskill and Caracelli, 1997, p. 215). Likewise, the *Guiding Principles for Evaluators* (American Evaluation Association, 1995, p. 25) tells us: "When planning and reporting evaluations, evaluators should consider including important perspectives and interests of the full range of stakeholders in the object being evaluated" (Principle E.1). And, the Joint Committee's (1994) first Utility Standard calls for the identification of "persons involved in or affected by the evaluation, . . . so that their needs can be addressed" (p. 25).

The number of stakeholders for any given evaluation can be daunting, however. Stakeholders have been variously described to include sponsors, funders, governing and advisory boards, policymakers, consumers, legislators, instructional and training staffs, administrators, staff members, service recipients, program developers, program participants, groups excluded from the program, community representatives, parents of service recipients, indirect beneficiaries, the general public, program beneficiaries, state and federal-level agency representatives, potential adopters, and community organizations (Joint Committee on Standards for Educational Evaluation, 1994; Mertens, 1998; Worthen, Sanders, and Fitzpatrick, 1997).

To what lengths should evaluators go in securing widely representative participation from these various groups—particularly when participation depends upon issues like (1) access to different stakeholders, (2) the political-organizational context, and (3) the time and resources available for conducting the evaluation? Is it a matter of violating ethical practice when an evaluator cannot garner what she believes to be adequately broad involvement? How are these situations resolved? Consider the following case:

A regional field office of a national nonprofit community service organization enlists an external consultant to evaluate one of its programs. This evaluator recently attended a workshop focusing on broad stakeholder involvement to encourage use. The particular approach she's learned recommends establishing an evaluation team consisting of stakeholders representing a broad spectrum of potential users of the evaluation's findings. This is a new approach for the evaluator who has previously focused on providing findings primarily for key decision makers. She is uncertain about which stakeholders from both within and outside the regional office to include on the team. She asks various managers for suggestions, but each of the seven she talks to insists they should be included. She tries to explain the importance of having program recipients, community members, program staff, other agency personnel, *as well as* some managers, represented. She also emphasizes the need to limit the size of the team to conduct the evaluation with a reasonable degree of efficiency, and to allow all groups the chance to voice their perspectives. Yet in spite of her pleas, they refuse to excuse themselves from the evaluation team, claiming that it's not important to involve outside groups because those groups don't make budgetary decisions about the program. The managers view the evaluation findings to be used primarily for allocating funds for the program in coming years.

The evaluator is very concerned that the managers will not represent a diversity of experiences and opinions about the program, that the evaluation findings will be less valid without wider participation, and therefore less useful for all concerned. She's worried that the managers will use their involvement as a means to pursue their political agendas relative to the program, which is becoming somewhat controversial within the community. Without other stakeholders present, the managers can shape the focus of the evaluation and even the data collection and interpretation of findings to meet their needs.

Here the evaluator is faced with a potential conflict between (1) an ethical commitment to broad stakeholder participation and (2) concerns for practicality and utility among the primary stakeholders. There are at least three possible outcomes to this case. First, the evaluator might persuade the managers of the value of having a diverse group of individuals on the evaluation team, arguing that they all hold information and perspectives critical to carrying out the evaluation successfully and that they are all potential users of the evaluation findings. As a result, they agree to a compromise whereby three of the seven managers remain on the team and other stakeholders are added. The evaluator is successful because she has begun to build trust, rapport, and credibility with the managers. Based on this developing personal power, she is able to help them understand the need for more diversity within the evaluation team. In so doing she has successfully resolved the ethical dilemma by balancing the need for broader stakeholder involvement and use to the primary audience.

In a second possible outcome the evaluator is unable to persuade the managers to change their position about all being on the team. She believes it is not worth excluding the managers considering their strong interest in participation. And since she is a consultant, she is concerned that there might also be some negative consequences to her reputation if she pushes too hard. She decides to enlarge the team to fifteen and includes other stakeholders. Still, she is concerned that managers not dominate the process. So as the team begins its work she stresses the need for equal participation for all members. At the same time though, she has additional worries that (1) the group's large size will slow the progress of the evaluation beyond when findings are needed, (2) the time required is more than team members can realistically give, and (3) her facilitation skills are not up to dealing with such a large group.

As it turns out, her fears are realized. Attendance within the team varies widely from meeting to meeting. Substantial time has to be spent at the beginning of each meeting bringing different members up to date. Further complicating matters, some of the team members who attend infrequently are beginning to raise issues within the community about the evaluation and how it is being conducted. The evaluator's dilemma is to balance needed stakeholder participation while maintaining credibility for the evaluation work within the group—whose participation is erratic.

A third outcome is that all seven managers remain on the evaluation team. The evaluator is unable to convince them of the value of wider participation. Later she attends the organization's national meeting, where she meets with other evaluators from the regional offices, some of whom attended the same evaluation workshop on stakeholder participation. As they are discussing the progress of their respective evaluations, she realizes that these evaluators have been much more successful at getting broad representation on their evaluation teams. Further, it is clear that the breadth of issues their evaluations addressed and their impact in the community are a reflection of this diverse representation. The evaluator is deeply troubled. She wonders whether she should have pushed harder, how her work will be viewed at the national level, and, even more important from an ethical standpoint, whether her community is being harmed in some way by the evaluation's narrow focus.

**How Should Stakeholders Be Involved?** The depth of stakeholders' participation can extend from problem identification, evaluation design, and development of data collection instruments to data collection, analysis, interpretation, and communicating and reporting findings. Depth of participation is determined by any number of variables, including stakeholders' availability, mutual expectations about roles, and stakeholders' technical knowledge and skill in evaluation methods. We are particularly concerned with the potential for ethical dilemmas arising when stakeholders participate extensively in the inquiry effort, as some evaluation and action research approaches advocate (for example, Fetterman, 1994; Heron, 1996; McTaggart, 1991; Preskill and Torres, 1999). Yet stakeholders may lack an appropriate level of technical skill in evaluation methods and practices.

Both the AEA Guiding Principles and the Joint Committee Standards identify evaluator competence as a key ethical issue. Principle B.1 states that "Evaluators should possess (or . . . ensure that the evaluation team possesses) the education, abilities, skills, and experience appropriate to undertake the tasks proposed in the evaluation" (American Evaluation Association, 1995, p. 22). Similarly, Standard U.2 (Joint Committee on Standards for Educational Evaluation, 1994) tells us that "the persons conducting the evaluation should be . . . competent to perform the evaluation, so that . . . findings achieve maximum credibility and acceptance" (p. 31).

Although involving stakeholders extensively may facilitate use, such involvement can be risky. What responsibility do evaluators have for assuring competent evaluation practice when stakeholders, who may be inexperienced in formal evaluation or social science inquiry, are actually conducting data collection and analysis activities? The following case of misuse, in which a stakeholder-evaluator reports prematurely on data before they are all collected and analyzed, focuses on this question.

The training department of a large business organized a team to evaluate a program for teaching employees how to access and use their new Intranet system. The Intranet is expected to increase learning and communication among organization members. Ultimately, company leaders believe it will help employees work more collaboratively and efficiently.

The team consists of five individuals from different departments (and different levels of responsibility) within the organization. They plan to conduct a pilot implementation and evaluation of the training program with a sample group of fifty employees. The methods of data collection the group decides to use include three focus group interviews at the end of the training and a post-training survey to be completed by all fifty pilot participants.

One of the evaluation team members volunteers to take responsibility for entering the survey data into a database. The two trainer-evaluators who chair the design and evaluation team and have more extensive experience in evaluation are pleased with this offer because it shows interest and commitment to the evaluation. The person who volunteered has the necessary skills for setting up a data base, entering the data, and carrying out appropriate statistical analyses.

However, as the surveys trickle in, this team member begins to share particular survey responses with other organization members. Much of what he is sharing focuses on some employees' dissatisfaction with aspects of the training experience. It is later revealed that this team member had not been particularly supportive of establishing the Intranet, and viewed these data as evidence that not only was the training ineffective, but that the implementation of the Intranet was not worth pursuing. As word spread throughout the organization that the training was a "failure," various managers began calling the training department expressing their displeasure with the trainers' work. As a result, the organization's management decides to scrub the training, and at considerable additional cost, hires an outside firm to develop and implement a company-wide Intranet training program. The employees who had participated in the pilot training were particularly dismayed because they had invested considerable time and effort in the pilot and its evaluation.

Yet when all of the data were finally analyzed, it was clear that overall, the training was considered effective by the majority of participants. The training staff and other team members wondered what they should have done differently.

In this case they faced a conflict between (1) the desire for meaningful participation and enhanced use among stakeholders and (2) ensuring the highest technical quality of the evaluation.

There are three possible ways this situation could have been avoided. First, the team leaders might have dealt more directly with the influence of different team members' attitudes and opinions on the validity of evaluation processes (in this case, on analysis and reporting). The Joint Committee's (1994) eleventh Accuracy Standard calls for "reporting procedures [that] guard against distortion caused by personal feelings and biases of any party to the evaluation, so that evaluation reports fairly reflect the evaluation findings" (p. 181). But the team leaders were not experienced at helping these stakeholders see how their underlying values, beliefs, and assumptions (whether supportive or unsupportive of the program) might influence their work on the evaluation. As a result, they were unable to prevent misuse of findings based on the promotion of self-interest (see Dial, 1994).

Second, the team leaders might have helped the group develop an evaluation plan that included appropriate implementation steps and timelines for data collection, analysis, and reporting. Also, they could have reviewed various aspects of good evaluation practice with these stakeholders, including ethics and standards in evaluation (Newman and Brown, 1996).

Finally, the team leaders could have consistently communicated the evaluation's progress to the managers, which might have preempted their early decision making. Had they been kept informed, managers might have questioned the preliminary data that were being circulated and not moved to act before all the data had been analyzed. Here the design and evaluation team leaders might not have prevented misuse in the first place, but would have contributed to "correct[ing] substantial misuses of their work" (American Evaluation Association, 1995).

## Mediating Factors in the Resolution of Ethical Challenges and Issues

Drawing on the cases just presented as well as relevant literature, the following discussion addresses three mediating factors in the occurrence and resolution of ethical challenges related to stakeholder participation and evaluation use.

**Evaluator Skills and Experience.** The literature on evaluation and related forms of action-oriented inquiry frequently calls for training evaluators in skills beyond technical expertise in research methods. These skills include organizational change, consultation and facilitation, gender and multicultural sensitivity, ethics and values (Mertens, 1998; Torres and others, 1996); knowledge of adult learning principles, instructional design, consultation and communication skills (Cousins and Earl, 1992); and group process and constructive confrontation skills (Greenwood and Levin, 1998).

As these cases illustrate, broader stakeholder participation can significantly increase the complexity of an evaluation endeavor. We feel that evaluators' effectiveness in dealing with potential ethical challenges is enhanced by their ability to sense and help redirect potential problems. In the final outcome of the stakeholder selection case, the evaluator lacked the interpersonal skills or experience to dissuade the organization's leadership from controlling the selection of stakeholders. The more skilled an evaluator is at sensing these kinds of potential problems and proactively addressing them, the less likely ethically problematic situations are to develop. Many seasoned evaluators can attest to the relationship between skill at avoiding or remediating ethical dilemmas and learning from past experience (see Morris and Cohn, 1993).

In the second case the trainer-evaluators had little experience in particular strategies they might use to engage stakeholders in dialogue to uncover potentially influential perspectives or biases. For instance, Posavac (1994) suggests asking stakeholders to imagine a favorable outcome and a possible negative outcome for conducting the evaluation. In addition to helping frame the evaluation study around issues of concern to stakeholders, this approach can provide individuals the opportunity to air underlying values, beliefs, and assumptions that might significantly influence their participation in the evaluation.

**Expectations for Stakeholder Participation.** Clearly, the two dimensions of stakeholder participation addressed here, selection and depth of participation, represent two continuums. In discussing stakeholder selection, Cousins and Whitmore (1998) suggest that a particular evaluation's position on the continuum depends on its purpose. That is, participatory evaluation undertaken for practical purposes (that is, to facilitate decision making) will include primary users (program sponsors, managers, developers, implementors), whereas participatory evaluation undertaken for transformative purposes (that is, to democratize social change) will include all legitimate groups, especially program beneficiaries. Likewise, depth of participation exists on a continuum, one endpoint of which involves stakeholders as equals in the conduct of the evaluation itself.

An increasing number of approaches to collaborative research and inquiry are being articulated, discussed, and practiced by evaluators (Cousins and Whitmore, 1998). As our profession matures, it is clear that existing ethics, standards, and guidelines cannot (nor were they intended to) give unequivocal guidance about whom to involve and in what way. More than ever, it is important for us as individual evaluators to clarify, for ourselves and among the stakeholders we seek to engage, what we believe about our work and the purposes it should serve.

How we view and deal with ethical dilemmas that arise in the course of our work can depend upon the philosophical underpinnings of the approaches we use and why we even chose to be evaluators. Evaluation codes of ethics are not explicit on the desired degree of stakeholder involvement or the trade-offs between various principles or standards. Individual evaluators will have different interpretations of the ethics of various approaches. In the first case presented here, the evaluator could have seen the managers as the primary users of the evaluation, included their input in the design of the evaluation, solicited the perspectives of a wider range of stakeholders through focus groups and/or surveys, and been satisfied that she had involved the different groups of stakeholders in the right ways. In fact, such an approach would satisfy both the Guiding Principle E.1 and the Joint Committee Standard U.1 pertaining to stakeholder involvement previously discussed. However, the depth of stakeholder participation in this instance might not be sufficient to maximize use of the evaluation. In contrast, another evaluator might have felt compelled "to raise the consciousness of the powerful people to include [more directly] those who have less power" (Mertens, 1998, p. 234).

House and Howe (1998) provide another example of how the evaluator's position on the purpose of the evaluation influences his or her perspective on potential ethical dilemmas. In their discussion of stakeholder inclusion they recognize that "the evaluator may be unduly influenced through extensive dialogue with various stakeholder groups," but "are willing to trade some threat to impartiality for the possibility of fully understanding stakeholder positions" (p. 4).

**Relationships with Stakeholders.**  Finally, we are continually reminded in our own evaluation practice of how our relationships with stakeholders influence success. As social scientists we have been, if not explicitly, implicitly encouraged to ignore the role that relationships play in the conduct of research and evaluation. Yet the more credibility, trust, rapport, and mutual understanding that exist between and among the participants in an evaluation endeavor, the more successful it seems to be. In the first outcome of the stakeholder selection case, the evaluator's capacity to persuade the managers is significantly enhanced by the credibility and trust she has been able to establish with them.

We are concerned with where and how these relationships will play out in the resolution of ethical dilemmas evaluators and stakeholders are certain to face. Will the pragmatic agenda for inquiry come into conflict with its relational dimensions? On the one hand, the nature of the ethical challenges we have presented in this chapter suggests that evaluators should (1) review and discuss the accepted principles of ethical evaluation practice with stakeholders, particularly those who will participate in the conduct of the evaluation itself; (2) receive initial and continuing training in process skills typically associated with consultation, organizational development, and instructional design and delivery; and (3) clarify their own and others' expectations for and understanding of what stakeholder participation means as it relates to the purpose of the evaluation.

On the other hand, we are impressed that as these evaluator-stakeholder relationships develop and flourish, we also may be influenced by an ethic of caring (see Noddings, 1996). As we seek to develop communities of inquiry whose work depends on the well being of the group, might our lens for viewing ethical evaluation practice be broadened in some way? We, like Schwandt (1998), wonder whether "knowing *through* relationships is something we ought to explore as an epistemology for an evaluation practice that is devoted to answering the questions: Are we doing the right thing, and are we doing it well?" (p. 11, italics in the original). Such questions can best be addressed through continued discourse among practicing evaluators who face the challenges and rewards of stakeholder participation.

# References

American Evaluation Association, Task Force on Guiding Principles for Evaluators. "Guiding Principles for Evaluators." In W. R. Shadish, D. L. Newman, M. A. Scheirer, and C. Wye (eds.), *Guiding Principles for Evaluators*. New Directions for Program Evaluation, no. 66. San Francisco: Jossey-Bass, 1995.

Cousins, J. B., Donohue, J. J., and Bloom, G. A. "Collaborative Evaluation in North America: Evaluators' Self-Reported Opinions, Practices and Consequences." *Evaluation Practice*, 1996, *17*, 207–226.

Cousins, J. B., and Earl, L. M. "The Case for Participatory Evaluation." *Educational Evaluation and Policy Analysis*, 1992, *14*, 397–418.

Cousins, J. B., and Earl, L. M. (eds.). *Participatory Evaluation in Education*. London: The Falmer Press, 1995.

Cousins, J. B., and Whitmore, E. "Framing Participatory Evaluation." In E. Whitmore (ed.), *Understanding and Practicing Participatory Evaluation*. New Directions for Evaluation, no. 80. San Francisco: Jossey-Bass, 1998.

Dial, M. "The Misuse of Evaluation in Educational Programs." In C. J. Stevens and M. Dial, (eds.), *Preventing the Misuse of Evaluation*. New Directions for Program Evaluation, no. 64. San Francisco: Jossey-Bass, 1994.

Fetterman, D. M. *Empowerment Evaluation*. Thousand Oaks, Calif.: Sage, 1994.

Greene, J. G. "Stakeholder Participation and Utilization in Program Evaluation." *Evaluation Review*, 1988, *12*, 91–116.

Greenwood, D. J., and Levin, M. *Introduction to Action Research: Social Research for Social Change*. Thousand Oaks, Calif.: Sage, 1998.

Guba, E., and Lincoln, Y. *Fourth Generation Evaluation*. Newbury Park, Calif.: Sage, 1989.

Heron, J. *Co-operative Inquiry: Research into the Human Condition*. Thousand Oaks, Calif.: Sage, 1996.

House, E. R., and Howe, K. R. "Deliberative Democratic Evaluation." Paper presented at the American Evaluation Association Conference, Chicago, November 1998.

Joint Committee on Standards for Educational Evaluation. *Standards for Evaluations of Educational Programs, Projects, and Materials.* New York: McGraw-Hill, 1981.

Joint Committee on Standards for Educational Evaluation. *The Program Evaluation Standards* (2nd ed.). Thousand Oaks, Calif.: Sage, 1994.

McTaggart, R. "When Democratic Evaluation Doesn't Seem Democratic." *Evaluation Practice,* 1991, 12, 9–21.

Mertens, D. *Research Methods in Education and Psychology.* Thousand Oaks, Calif.: Sage, 1998.

Morris, M., and Cohn, R. "Program Evaluators and Ethical Challenges: A National Survey." *Evaluation Review,* 1993, 17, 621–642.

Newman, D. L., and Brown, R. D. *Applied Ethics for Program Evaluation.* Thousand Oaks, Calif.: Sage, 1996.

Noddings, N. "On Community." *Educational Theory,* 1996, 46, 245–267.

O'Sullivan, R. G., and O'Sullivan, J. M. "Evaluation Voices: Promoting Evaluation from within Programs through Collaboration." *Evaluation and Program Planning,* 1998, 21, 21–29.

Patton, M. Q. *Utilization-Focused Evaluation: The New Century Text.* (3rd ed.) Thousand Oaks, Calif.: Sage, 1997.

Posavac, E. J. "Misusing Program Evaluation by Asking the Wrong Question." In C. J. Sevens and M. Dial (eds.), *Preventing the Misuse of Evaluation.* New Directions for Program Evaluation, no. 64. San Francisco: Jossey-Bass, 1994.

Preskill, H., and Caracelli, V. "Current and Developing Conceptions of Use: Evaluation Use TIG Survey Results." *Evaluation Practice,* 1997, 18, 209–225.

Preskill, H., and Torres, R. T. *Evaluative Inquiry for Learning in Organizations.* Thousand Oaks, Calif.: Sage, 1999.

Schwandt, T. A. "How We Think about Morality: Implications for Evaluation Practice." Paper presented at the American Evaluation Association Conference, Chicago, November 1998.

Shulha, L. "Learning to Participate in Participatory Evaluation: A Case Study in the Transformation of Design." Paper presented at the American Evaluation Association Conference, Vancouver, B.C., November 1994.

Stake, R. E., and Mabry, L. "Ethics in Program Evaluation." Paper delivered at the conference, "Evaluation as a Tool in the Development of Social Work Discourse," Stockholm, April 1997.

Torres, R. T., Preskill, H. S., and Piontek, M. *Evaluation Strategies for Communicating and Reporting: Enhancing Learning in Organizations.* Thousand Oaks, Calif.: Sage, 1996.

Worthen, B. R., Sanders, J. R., and Fitzpatrick, J. *Program Evaluation.* New York: Longman, 1997.

*ROSALIE T. TORRES is director of research and evaluation at the Developmental Studies Center (DSC) in Oakland, California. She facilitates an organizational learning approach to the evaluation of DSC's programs. DSC is a nonprofit educational organization that develops programs and materials to help elementary schools strengthen children's social, ethical, and intellectual development.*

*HALLIE PRESKILL is associate professor at the University of New Mexico and program coordinator of the organizational learning and instructional technologies graduate program. She continues to be intrigued with and fascinated by evaluative inquiry and organizational learning.*

*For ethics to become an integrated component of the discipline of evaluation, education in ethics must become part of evaluation training. This chapter initiates a discussion on ethics education, including what should be taught and who should receive the training.*

# Education and Training in Evaluation Ethics

*Dianna L. Newman*

The environments in which we practice evaluation are presenting an increasing number of ethical challenges. Continued devolution, decentralization, and privatization of social, education, and health programs are expanding the number of ethical dilemmas faced by evaluators. Unlike other professions, such as law, medicine, and accounting, we have done little to incorporate ethics into our training. Though we have adopted a set of ethical guidelines, until they become part of our common training and practice, it is questionable whether we truly have a set of "common" ethics.

This chapter addresses issues pertaining to the transmittal of common ethical values related to the practice of evaluation. The issues discussed include the need for development and adoption of a common or core set of knowledge of ethics in evaluation; the need to provide this knowledge to all evaluation participants, including the evaluator, the client, and the consumer; and the need for the development of multiple methods of instruction and assessment.

## The Search for a Core Curriculum

If ethics are to become a part of our evaluation culture, we must identify the core ethical concepts that should be included in evaluation training and practice. Identifying these concepts will move us toward establishing a common curriculum in evaluation ethics that can be used to educate evaluators, clients, and consumers. As a means of facilitating the development of this core area, I recommend four content domains for consideration: (1) the foundation of ethical systems, (2) existing written ethical codes, (3) guidelines for the daily use of ethics, and (4) intervening variables affecting ethical practice. Following is a brief discussion of the suggested curriculum content for each area. A summary of these topics is provided in Exhibit 7.1.

**Foundation of Ethical Systems.** This curriculum domain serves two major goals: first, to provide knowledge to students on the theories and assumptions underlying the development and use of ethical codes; second, to encourage students to think reflectively about their own beliefs about ethics. Three major content areas facilitate these goals:

*Philosophies of Ethics.* This content includes an overview of major philosophies underlying ethical processes. The philosophies most relevant to the practice of evaluation are the ethics of consequence, duty, rights, social justice, and caring. Further, these philosophies are prevalent in evaluation literature.

The ethic of consequence, with modern roots in the writings of Bentham ([1789] 1970), Hume ([1751] 1983), and Mill ([1863] 1962), emphasizes utility and outcomes. According to this philosophy, the rightness of a decision is based on one's perception of its consequence or utility. On the one hand, evaluators using this approach will place a priority on evaluation processes that verify client-specified outcomes because they are perceived as having the greatest utility. This philosophy underlies much of early evaluation practice. On the other hand, evaluators advocating duty, obligation, and means instead of end use are supportive of a deontological philosophy (Kant, [1788] 1956). They

### Exhibit 7.1. Suggested Core Curriculum in Ethics of Evaluation

I. The Background of Ethical Systems
   1. Philosophies of Ethics (the ethics of consequence, duty, right, social justice, and caring)
   2. Common Principles Related to Ethical Practice in Western Culture (autonomy, nonmaleficence, beneficence, justice, and fidelity)
   3. Conflicts in Ethical Decision Making
II. A Working Knowledge of Existing Written Ethical Codes
   1. American Evaluation Association: Guiding Principles for Evaluators
   2. Joint Committee on Standards for Evaluation: Program Evaluation and Personnel Evaluation
   3. Discipline-Based Standards
III. Guidelines for Daily Use of Ethics
   1. A Decision-Making Framework
   2. Asking Questions about Ethical Practice
   3. Monitoring Ethical Practice
IV. Intervening Variables Affecting Ethical Practice
   1. Roles of Evaluators
   2. Internal and External Evaluation
   3. Policy and Politics
   4. Alternative Approaches to Evaluation

believe that the rightness of actions is not determined by their outcomes but by a comparison of the selected action with a broader set of actions that might be appropriate for multiple settings. Determining that a program does or does not meet the client's proposed objectives may not be considered adequate practice in this case if the evaluator knows that the program is limited in scope or that better measures of outcomes are available.

Human rights-based philosophy stresses the belief that all people have value and must be treated with dignity and respect. Evaluators who advocate this philosophy place priority on stakeholders' rights to privacy and dignity over the need to collect data affirming program objectives. Social justice philosophy expands and builds upon the rights of individuals to address needs of groups or society. In advocating social justice, Rawls (1971) proposed two basic principles: (1) everyone has an equal right to basic liberties, and (2) efforts to combat inequities should assist the least advantaged first. House (1991, 1993) is a proponent of social justice in evaluation settings and argues that evaluators may need to go beyond the traditional boundaries set for evaluation methods and use to include and, if need be, advocate for the powerless stakeholder.

The ethics of care also has become an important component of evaluation literature. This perspective (Mertens, 1994; Ryan, 1994) emphasizes greater attention to the relationships and context of the program, the evaluator, and, if appropriate, the ethical dilemma. This approach is congruent with Lincoln and Guba's (1989) Fourth Generation perspective of evaluation as well as Schwandt's (1992) view of the evaluator as a reflective practitioner.

Newman and Brown (1996) present a more detailed summary of these philosophies, emphasizing the similarities and differences of their underlying assumptions, their relationship to evaluation practice, how they affect decisions pertaining to evaluation planning, and their impact on evaluation use.

*Common Principles Related to Ethical Practice in Western Culture.* This curriculum content includes an overview of five ethical principles identified by Kitchner (1984, 1985) as most frequently present in professional standards in Western culture. These principles connect to the ethical philosophies identified above to the evaluation context.

The first of these principles, autonomy, reflects the right to act independently and to make one's own choices; it also includes the obligation to allow others to act independently and to make their own choices. For example, although an evaluator should have the autonomy to collect and report data from multiple stakeholders, clients should have the autonomy of weighing those findings according to their own perceptions of the decision-making context.

The second principal, nonmaleficence, includes the duty to do no undue harm, that is, to avoid actions that might unduly hurt others. In evaluation it is important to stress the use of the word "undue" when speaking of harm. All evaluations can be said to have some form of negative consequences; the ethical emphasis is on avoiding undue harm. For instance, if a program is not functioning properly it is the duty of the evaluator to notify the client of this finding, but the notification does not need to be done in such a way that consumers of the program are left without any services.

Beneficence, or benefiting others, goes beyond the ethics of avoiding harm and emphasizes helping others beyond the normal expectations. Among evaluators, beneficence could include assisting clients in redefining outcome measures, advocating for the inclusion of disempowered stakeholders, and following up on report use.

Justice, as a principle, reflects objectivity, impartiality, and equal treatment; it also concerns reacting to and including program clients and consumers in the evaluation process in a way that is equitable to all. Justice implies that evaluators have respect for individual rights and a sense of value for all stakeholders. Highest priority is placed on maintaining the personal rights of all participants.

The principle of fidelity concerns loyalty and honesty to a larger group. It includes being faithful and fulfilling implicit and explicit obligations. In evaluation, conflicts can arise around the recipient of an evaluator's loyalty. For example, whose need for information is paramount, clients' or stakeholders'? Do we owe greater obligations to our profession or to our employer? Conflicts concerning honesty also are evident in debates concerning the validity and accuracy of data, the selection of information found in reports, and distribution of findings.

*Conflicts in Ethical Decision Making.* This section of the curriculum should acknowledge the multifaceted, conflicting culture of ethics. It should be practice based with a goal of assisting students in reflecting on their own ethical philosophy and their use of principles to justify their actions. Students should be provided with "real-life" evaluation situations in which ethical dilemmas have occurred. Through analysis of these cases they should gain an appreciation of the different opinions others can legitimately hold and, hence, the ambiguity of some ethical dimensions. They should also gain an appreciation of the lack of "right" or "wrong" responses and the need to acknowledge their own and others' varied perceptions. At the conclusion of this section, students should be ready to acknowledge the need for evaluation-specific codes of ethics and the need to develop a decision-making framework based on codes, principles, and philosophies of ethics that they can call on when involved in ethical conflicts.

**Existing Written Ethical Codes.** The purpose of this curriculum unit is to provide students with a working knowledge of existing written ethical codes that encompass evaluation. Codes reviewed would include "The Guiding Principles for Evaluators" (American Evaluation Association, 1995), the Joint Committee's *Program Evaluation Standards* (1994) and *Personnel Evaluation Standards* (1988), and program content or discipline-based standards. Knowledge of the latter codes, such as those of the American Psychological Association or the American Educational Research Association, allow students to become familiar with the various discipline-based standards that may be guiding the decision making of their evaluation clients and consumers. Additional written policies that should be reviewed include the use of internal review boards and institutional review policies. When studying this material, students should be given opportunities to compare and contrast various decisions and outcomes that might result from differing uses or interpretations of written documents.

**Guidelines for the Daily Use of Ethics.** Using ethics in daily practice includes weighing the decisions that we make in planning, conducting, reporting, and using evaluation so that maximum good can occur while protecting the rights of all stakeholders throughout the process. One of the goals of this unit is to provide students with a framework for addressing ethical decisions that occur on a daily basis. Using the knowledge of ethical philosophies, principles, and written standards gained in the earlier components, students should become able to identify, discuss, and arrive at possible solutions to ethical conflicts.

Newman and Brown (1996) provide a framework for daily use. In this framework, evaluators proceed through five levels of question and decision-making options. These levels include using their own intuition, using current sets of ethical rules or standards, reviewing the conflict in light of ethical principles and philosophies, evaluating the dilemma in terms of their own personal values, and ultimately generating a list of possible actions. These actions are then weighed in terms of the context of the evaluation, obligations to employees or clients, loyalty to the profession, and the good of the greater community. Throughout the process, the model stresses the need to communicate with other evaluators and to solicit and weigh alternative options.

A second goal of the daily practice unit is to prepare students, as members of a profession, to question their own and others' ethical beliefs as exemplified in practice and theory and to become contributors to the development of a more defined common culture of ethical practice. Potential topics for this unit include acknowledgment of the role of personal values, need for rules versus need for ethics, actions and reactions that can result from ethical questioning, and the need for continued growth and education in ethical practice.

The last focus of the unit on daily use should be monitoring ethical practice in evaluation. Emphasis should be placed on self-monitoring, peer monitoring, monitoring by professional organizations, and monitoring by clients and consumers. Students should become familiar with alternative methods and levels of monitoring ethical practice and the pros and cons associated with each method and level. Students also should be encouraged to participate in the development of more effective means of assessing ethical practice.

**Intervening Variables That May Affect Ethical Decision Making.** This section of the curriculum, building on the knowledge base presented above, allows students to address issues unique to evaluation practice such as the multiple roles of the evaluator, the impact of politics and policy on evaluation, the internal or external status of the evaluator, and specific practices associated with the approach to evaluation. Newman and Brown (1996) identify five major roles of evaluators that can cause ethical conflicts: evaluator as consultant/administrator, evaluator as data collector/researcher, evaluator as reporter, evaluator as a member of a profession, and evaluator as a member of society.

Mathison (1991) complements and expands the concept of ethical issues related to the role of an evaluator, differentiating between the conflicts commonly associated with the practice of external evaluators and those of internal evaluators. Ethical decision making in evaluation is also influenced by policy changes. Federal and state mandates concerning the practice of evaluation may pose ethical dilemmas. Examples of such changes include current mandates to provide summative data on short-term program implementation, requests for more intrusive data as a means of documenting program effects, and the required inclusion of advocate groups in the evaluation process. Other intervening variables include organizational policies and procedures and variations in practice caused by the method of evaluation. The latter could include decision-making models compared to participatory models, quantitative methods compared to qualitative methods, and the impact of advocacy evaluation. Chelimsky and Shadish (1997) provide a summary of some of these issues.

## Who Should We Train?

When considering the "whom" of ethics education, Newman (1996) identified three major stakeholders who should be considered. These include those who do evaluations, those who commission evaluations, and those who are consumers of what is being evaluated.

Of major importance is the need to educate evaluators on the ethics of practice. These students include new evaluators, practicing evaluators, and part-time evaluators. Multiple programs throughout the country are now offering pre-service education in evaluation (Altschuld and Engle, 1994), but it is unclear to what extent students are trained in the ethics of practice. Training also must be provided to those who will consider evaluation to be a secondary area of their professional practice. Many part-time evaluators receive only methodological training with, at most, an overview of evaluation theory. Many will not become a member of a professional evaluation organization, and many are not aware of the ethical obligations that the terms "evaluator" and "evaluation" convey. The special need for continuing education to current, practicing evaluators also must be addressed. The majority of evaluators who will practice for the next thirty years have already received their formal training. Certification and accreditation programs will alleviate some of these difficulties but only if the ethics of practice is included in the review and only if the review encompasses more than the ethical practice of inquiry within the student's primary discipline.

The second group of students, clients who commission evaluations, must be educated on what they can and should expect as ethical practice on the part of the evaluator they hire. Many professional training programs, for example, educational administration and counseling psychology, are beginning to include the concept of program evaluation within their own curriculum. This training should include not only how to be an evaluator but also how to be a client or consumer of evaluation.

The third group of students are those who receive the services offered by the program being evaluated. These consumers will be harder to access, but represent those who are the most vulnerable to the consequences of unethical practice. More inclusive, contextually based approaches to education will have to be developed to reach these students. For instance, advocacy training for parents of children with disabilities could include not only how to advocate directly for services, but how to be sure that parents' voices are heard as part of the evaluation of services.

This training of clients, staff, and consumers becomes increasingly important as evaluators use stakeholder, participatory, and empowerment evaluation. Research has shown that inclusion of these stakeholders is not as easy as first thought (Newman, Singer, and Osuna, 1997). There appears to be a pattern of developmental growth in involvement that is related to both willingness and opportunity to be involved and prior experience in evaluation. Newman and Lobosco (1997) delineate a multistage developmental model of involvement in participatory evaluation that identifies knowledge of ethical practice as a major characteristic for active inclusion. They then document three levels of ethical knowledge that reflect parallel levels of participation.

## Providing the Training: Instructional Issues

Once a common core of knowledge pertaining to ethics and evaluation is established, we must develop the means of imparting this knowledge. For the past several years, the American Evaluation Association has encouraged teachers of evaluation to share exemplary practices in teaching evaluation concepts, including standards for the practice of evaluation and the ethics of evaluation. (See, as examples, Sanders, Newman, Owen, and Worthen, 1996, and Newman, 1996.) In addition, several special issues have been published that pertain to the ethics of evaluation (see, for example, *Evaluation and Program Planning,* 8, 1985) and the teaching of evaluation (Altschuld and Engle, 1994), including the ethics of practice. Several authors, including Newman (1995), Mertens (1994), and Morris and Cohn (1993), have called for the inclusion of more training on ethics for evaluators in both formal and informal settings. As a result, several instructional strategies exist that can be used to model conveying and sharing of information about ethical practice in evaluation. Proven strategies include analysis of individual case studies, direct instruction of standards and principles, interactive learning while on projects, reflective journal analysis, stand-alone presentations, and group review. Several authors (Brown, 1985; Newman and Lobosco, 1997) have developed frameworks for working with students in evaluation settings that reflect a developmental approach to learning evaluation, including ethics, and suggest alternative teaching strategies that meet a variety of levels of learning. These strategies include directive, collaborative, and learner-guided approaches (Lobosco and Newman, 1998), as well as varied levels of hands-on learning ranging from involvement in role playing, through supervised practicum participation, to autonomous internship activities.

**Assessment.** At present, there is little, if any, information available on how we should assess stakeholders' knowledge of and ability to practice ethical evaluation. It is imperative that we develop means of evaluating our written ethical codes, the training we provide on their use, and their subsequent use in practice. We must develop a systematic means of assessing their utility, feasibility, and value in both the abstract and practical sense. This will not be an easy process. Areas in need of discussion include the depth of formal assessment that is needed, methods of assessing the assimilation of socialized values, the need to provide peer assessment as well as expert assessment, the need for continued assessment, and the role of assessment of ethical knowledge and practice within accreditation, certification, and degree-granting programs.

As an initial effort in this development, I suggest that evaluation theorists and educators, using both case study and practitioner-generated approaches, begin investigating alternative assessment methods for which assumptions of both philosophical and psychometric properties are evident. These beginning efforts may result initially in low-level assessments of knowledge and practice, but will provide formative information on the varied interpretations of our practice and will identify areas in which there is a lack of agreement. Subsequent development of assessment methods could rely less on measurement of factual information, instead emphasizing the use of appropriate processes of ethical decision-making and strategies.

## Summary

This chapter calls first for the development of a common or core curriculum in ethics that can be used when providing knowledge to evaluators, clients, and consumers. This core must be adaptable to both pre-service and in-service training in a variety of educational settings. Increased emphasis also is needed in development of assessment methodologies for both our codes of ethics and our use of these codes. As evaluation advances in professional status, the knowledge and use of ethics will continue to require theorists and practitioners to make thoughtful interpretations. The quality of these interpretations depends on making ethics a key component of training in evaluation.

## References

Altschuld, J. W., and Engle, M. (eds.). *The Preparation of Professional Evaluators: Issues, Perspectives, and Programs.* New Directions for Program Evaluation, no. 62. San Francisco: Jossey-Bass, 1994.

American Evaluation Association, Task Force on Guiding Principles for Evaluators. "Guiding Principles for Evaluators." In W. R. Shadish, D. L. Newman, M. A. Scheirer, and C. Wye (eds.), *Guiding Principles for Evaluators.* New Directions for Program Evaluation, no. 66. San Francisco, Jossey-Bass, 1995.

Bentham, J. "An Introduction to the Principles of Morals and Legislation." J. M. Burns and H. L. A. Hart (eds.). London: Atholone, 1970. (Originally published 1789.)

Brown, R. D. "Supervising Evaluation Practium and Intern Students: A Developmental Model." *Educational Evaluation and Policy Analysis,* 1985, *2,* 161–167.

Chelimsky, E., and Shadish, W. R. (eds.). *Evaluation for the 21st Century: A Handbook.* Thousand Oaks, Calif.: Sage, 1997.

House, E.R. "Evaluation and Social Justice: Where Are We?" In M. W. McLaughlin and D. C. Philips (Eds.), *Evaluation and Education: At Quarter Century.* Chicago: University of Chicago Press, 1991.

House, E. R. *Professional Evaluation: Social Impact and Political Consequences.* Newbury Park, Calif.: Sage, 1993.

Hume, D. "Enquiry Concerning the Principles of Morals." J. B. Schneewind (ed.). Indianapolis, Ind.: Hackett, 1983. (Originally published 1751.)

Joint Committee on Standards for Educational Evaluation. *Personnel Evaluation Standards.* Newbury Park, Calif.: Sage Publications, 1988.

Joint Committee on Standards for Educational Evaluation. *The Program Evaluation Standards.* Thousand Oaks, Calif.: Sage Publications, 1994.

Kant, I. "Critique of Practical Reason." In L. W. Beck (Trans.), *Critique of Practical Reason.* New York: Liberal Arts Press, 1956. (Originally published 1788.)

Kitchner, K. S. "Intuition, Critical Evaluation and Ethical Principles: The Foundation for Ethical Decisions in Counseling Psychology." *The Counseling Psychologist,* 1984, *12* (3), 43–56.

Kitchner, K. S. "Ethical Principles and Ethical Decisions in Student Affairs." In H. S. Cannon and R. D. Brown (ed.), *Applied Ethics in Student Affairs.* New Directions for Student Services, no. 30. San Francisco: Jossey-Bass, 1985.

Lincoln, Y. S., and Guba, E. G. "Ethics: The Failure of Positivist Science." *Review of Higher Education,* 1989, *12* (3), 221–240.

Lobosco, A. F., and Newman, D. L. "Working Effectively with Program Stakeholders in Participatory Evaluation." Paper presented at the Annual Meeting of the American Evaluation Association, Chicago, November, 1998.

Mathison, S. "Role Conflicts for Internal Evaluators." *Evaluation and Program Planning,* 1991, *14,* 173–179.

Mertens, D. M. "Implications for Evaluation Practice from a Multicultural, Feminist Perspective on Ethics." Paper presented at the annual meeting of the American Evaluation Association, Boston, November 1994.

Mertens, D. M. "Training Evaluators: Unique Skills and Knowledge." In J.W. Altschuld and M. Engle (eds.), The Preparation of Professional Evaluators: Issues, Perspectives, and Programs. *New Directions for Program Evaluation,* no. 66. San Francisco: Jossey-Bass, 1994.

Mill, J. S. "Utilitarianism: On Liberty." In M. Warnock (ed.), *On Liberty.* Cleveland, Ohio: World, 1962. (Originally published 1863.)

Morris M., and Cohn, R. "Program Evaluators and Ethical Challenges: A National Survey." *Evaluation Review,* 1993, *17* (6), 621–642.

Newman, D. L. "The Future of Ethics in Evaluation: Developing the Dialogue." In W. R. Stadish, D. L. Newman, M. A. Schurer, and C. Wye (eds.), *Guiding Principles for Evaluators.* New Directions for Program Evaluation, no. 66. San Francisco: Jossey-Bass, 1995.

Newman, D. L. "Teaching Ethics in Program Evaluation: Advancing the Profession." Paper presented at the Annual Meeting of the American Evaluation Association, Atlanta, November 1996.

Newman, D. L., and Brown, R. D. *Applied Ethics in Program Evaluation.* Thousand Oaks, Calif.: Sage Publications, 1996.

Newman, D. L., and Lobosco, A. F. "A Developmental Approach to Participatory Evaluation." Paper presented at the Annual Meeting of the American Evaluation Association, San Diego, November 1997.

Newman, D. L., Singer, M., and Osuna, M. "Expanding the Participatory Model: Case Studies in Real Use of Participatory Evaluation." Paper presented at the Annual Meeting of the American Evaluation Association, San Diego, November 1997.

Rawls, J. *A Theory of Justice.* Cambridge, Mass.: Belknap Press of Harvard University Press, 1971.

Ryan, K. E. "Using Feminist Strategies for Addressing Issues of Social Justice: Do They Help?" Paper presented at the annual meeting of the American Evaluation Association, November 1994.

Sanders, J. R., Newman, D. L., Owen, J., and Worthen, B. "Making the Program Evaluation Standards Meaningful in Graduate Education." Panel presented at the Annual Meeting of the American Evaluation Association, Atlanta, November, 1996.

Schwandt, T. A. "Better Living Through Evaluation: Images of Progress Shaping Evaluation Practice." *Evaluation Practice,* 1992, *13* (2), 135–144.

DIANNA L. NEWMAN *is associate professor and director of the Evaluation Consortium at the State University of New York at Albany. She is coauthor of Applied Ethics in Program Evaluation, and "Guiding Principles for Evaluators" and has presented and published numerous papers and articles on ethics in evaluation. She is currently working on a developmental model of training evaluators that encompasses knowledge as well as experience.*

*Few ethical issues seem to arouse the passion generated by discussions of whether or when evaluators should be advocates, adversaries, or neutral in light of the social goals that programs seek to achieve. The arguments for and against evaluation advocacy are examined in terms of the American Evaluation Association's "Guiding Principles for Evaluators," more recent statements on advocacy and neutrality, and one aspect of practice: "closeness" to intended beneficiaries. The conclusion? It is time for a revised definition of Guiding Principle C (Integrity/Honesty), one that more effectively reflects our common ground and permits better articulation of standards.*

# The Ethics of Evaluation Neutrality and Advocacy

*Lois-ellin Datta*

Violence against clinics and medical personnel performing abortions has increased. The federal government has increased the penalties against the perpetrators and also has taken other measures. An evaluation team gathers to assess the effectiveness of these measures. One member of the team, like many others in this nation, is strongly "pro-life," believing that under the Nuremberg and other rulings, any action is justified in preventing what this person regards as the slaughter of innocents. This team member sees the government as protecting "murderers," believing the general welfare and public good demand closure of the clinics. Another team member, like many others in this nation, is strongly "pro-choice," believing that law and ethics give a woman control over her own body and regarding violence against the clinics and medical personnel as criminal, not heroic. To this team member, ensuring the general welfare and public good requires the protection of clinics offering abortions. Both members call themselves evaluators. Should either of these evaluators participate in or lead the evaluation?

For this chapter, I have been asked to examine arguments for and against evaluation neutrality and advocacy. To explore these issues I have looked primarily at articles by past presidents of the American Evaluation Association and other prominent figures in our field. There is an abundance of prior words on this topic, some of which will be summarized in the next sections. Sorting through them, what struck me was not their dissimilarity but—with some exceptions—their agreement after one had worked through the definitions given of advocacy and neutrality. Nonetheless, some of the discourse on the ethics of advocacy in evaluation seems to take place as though the moral high ground had room for only one banner.

Why the passion, given the common ground? One reason may be the potential for common ground in theory to get "balkanized" in practice. A second

NEW DIRECTIONS FOR EVALUATION, no. 82, Summer 1999 © Jossey-Bass Publishers reason may be whether the evaluator primarily has in mind a national study or one close to client service delivery. The explanatory power of this distinction, granted, does not always hold. Without deprecating the many ethical and moral dilemmas confronting evaluators, perhaps we could advance a bit further by examining (1) specific evaluations carried out at *comparable levels* in light of (2) the principles and theories put forth under different banners.

## Guiding Principles for Evaluators

Our starting point is the "Guiding Principles for Evaluators" adopted by the American Evaluation Association (AEA) as "a set of principles that should guide the professional practice of evaluations, and that should inform evaluation clients and the general public about the principles they can expect to be upheld by professional evaluators" (American Evaluation Association, 1995, p. 21). There are five broad principles: systematic inquiry, competence, integrity/honesty, respect for people, and responsibilities for general and public welfare. These have been presented earlier in this volume.

All of the AEA Guiding Principles are relevant, to some degree, to the ethics of advocacy. One cannot, however, scan the principles for general guidance regarding advocacy and know exactly what actions to take. First, as intended, the principles are not standards. They do not indicate, for example, matters of practice, such as what would constitute incompetent performance or what types of education, abilities, skills, and experience would be inappropriate for different types of evaluation tasks for different evaluations. Second, it is possible for persons taking different positions on the ethics of advocacy or neutrality in evaluation to cite one or another principle as consistent with their views.

In the next sections, these apparently dissimilar positions are presented together with the AEA Guiding Principles that seem to support them, and then the positions are reexamined to identify what may be common ground that redefines the Principles. First, four definitions (Webster's, 1994):

> Advocate: One who defends, vindicates, or espouses a cause by argument; upholder; defender; one who pleads for or in behalf of another
> Adversary: A person or group who opposes another; opponent; foe; any enemy who fights determinedly, relentlessly, continuously
> Partisan: An adherent or supporter of a person, party, or cause; biased; partial
> Nonpartisan: Objective; not supporting any of the established or regular parties

## To Evaluate Requires Credibility: No, Evaluators Should Not Be Advocates

There is no lack of words and deeds concerning what evaluation and the evaluator's role are about. Some could be read as indicating that the evaluator's role is about creating nonpartisan evaluations regardless of how partisan or nonpartisan the world itself may be.

For example, Chelimsky (1997) observes:

> To be listened to by various stakeholders in even an ordinary political debate requires a great deal of effort by evaluators not only to be competent and objective but to appear so. . . . There are. . . a great many things we can do. . . not just technically, in the steps we take to make and explain our evaluative decisions, but also intellectually, in the effort we put forth to look at all sides and stakeholders in an evaluation. . . . A second implication for evaluators of a political environment is the need for courage. . . . Speaking out in situations that may include numerous political adversaries, all with different viewpoints and axes to grind, and also insisting on the right to independence in speaking out, takes a strong stomach. . . . It takes courage to refuse sponsors the answers they want to hear, to resist becoming a "member of the team," to fight inappropriate intrusion into the evaluation process . . . but when courage is lost, everything is lost. [pp. 57–60; see also Cook, 1997]

This is Scriven (1997):

> Distancing can be thought of as a scale on which a number of points are of particular interest. . . . At one end of the scale is complete distancing, as when a program (person, policy, or whatever) is evaluated on the basis of extant data alone. At the other end is ownership or authorship of the program, usually conceded to be a poor basis for objective evaluation of it. . . . Although it is better in principle to use extant data, it is often the case that one needs more, and the risks attendant on personal involvement [bias] must be undertaken. . . . So-called participatory design, part of the empowerment movement, is about as sloppy as one can get, short of participatory authoring of the final report (unless that report is mainly done for educational or therapeutic purposes). . . . It is sometimes suggested that the push for distance is itself an attempt to be superior, external, an attempt to play God the Judge. On the contrary, it is part of the simple and sensible human effort to get things right, to uncover and report the truth—Deciding when and to what extent to withhold those findings from those who paid for them is the "doing what's good for you, not what you asked me to do" step over the border between expertise and censorship/parenting. [pp. 484, 491]

## To Evaluate Is to Advocate: Yes, Evaluators Should Be Advocates

Other work could be read as saying we are about creating partisan evaluations in an irretrievably partisan world. We should be advocates, weighing in on the side of the underdog, the oppressed, the marginalized in the fight for social justice.

Lincoln (1990) writes, "[To the positivists], only if research results were free of human values, and, therefore, free from bias, prejudice, or individual stakes could social action be taken that was neutral with respect to political partisanship. . . . The constructivist paradigm [has as its central focus] . . . the presentation of multiple, holistic, competing and often conflictual realities of multiple stakeholders and research participants . . . the written report should demonstrate the passion, the commitment, and the involvement of the inquirer with his or her coparticipants in the inquiry" (pp. 70–71). She further comments, "We should abandon the role of dispassionate observer in favor of the role of passionate participant" (p. 86).

Greene (1995), expanding on this thought, urges in her classic, widely cited article, "Evaluation inherently involves advocacy, so the important question becomes advocacy for whom. The most defensible answer to this question is that evaluation should advocate for the interests of the participants" (p. 1). In a related statement, Fetterman (1997) offers a nuanced argument, considering both advocacy and data credibility, that evaluation is best seen as a form of empowerment. He observes, "Empowerment evaluation has an unambiguous value orientation—it is designed to help people help themselves and improve their programs, using a form of self-evaluation and reflection. . . . Advocacy, in this context, becomes a natural by-product of the self-evaluation process—if the data merit it" (pp. 382–384).

And Mertens (1995):

> This principle (III.D.5) concerning diversity and inclusion has implications not only at the level of identifying and respecting the viewpoints of marginalized groups, but also for the technical adequacy of what evaluators do. . . . Evaluators need to reflect on how to address validity and reliability honestly in a cultural context, so as not to violate the human rights of the culturally oppressed. . . . [The emancipatory framework] . . . is more appropriate to stop oppression and bring about social justice. Three characteristics [of this framework are] (1) recognition of silenced voices, ensuring that groups traditionally marginalized in society are equally "heard" during the evaluation process and formation of evaluation findings and recommendations; (2) analysis of power inequities in terms of social relationships involved in the planning, implementation, and reporting of evaluations; (3) linking evaluation results to political action. [pp. 91–92].

In the context of evaluation as advocacy, stakeholder involvement seems to mean the evaluator should take up the cause of the marginalized. The evaluator should make or support procedural, technical, and methodological decisions favoring the side of the persons directly receiving services.

## Some Relevant Principles and Their Implications for Anti- and Pro-Advocacy Stances

The AEA Guiding Principles do not rule out either the anti-advocacy or pro-advocacy stances, and various ones can be cited to support either position.

**Against Advocacy.** Several of the AEA Guiding Principles can be cited to emphasize the incompatibility of evaluation with an advocacy position as indicated in the quotes given. These are found primarily under Principle C: Integrity/Honesty. In its subparts, this principle emphasizes that evaluators should assure the honesty and integrity of the entire evaluation process through practices such as being explicit about their own (and others') interests concerning the conduct and outcome of evaluations, disclosing any roles or relationships that might pose a significant conflict of interest.

As these words are generally understood, they are inconsistent with an advocacy position. According to Webster's (1994), *honest* means "Honorable in principles, intentions, actions; fair; genuine or unadulterated; truthful or creditable; unadorned; just, incorruptible, trustworthy; truthful; straight forward, candid." In common understanding, as an evaluator one cannot be fair to all stakeholders and at the same time take a position of advocacy (or adversary) for or against one stakeholder group or the other. The principles tell us to be scrupulous about identifying biases, values, preconceptions favoring one outcome or another that may be held so strongly the evaluator could find it difficult to be fair, incorruptible, just, trustworthy. These threats to fairness specifically and explicitly included political stances. That is, the principles assume that evaluators have biases, prejudices, values, opinions. They require us, however, to be ever mindful of how our values may affect our conduct of the evaluation—and to disqualify ourselves from a particular study if we cannot be balanced, fair, just, incorruptible.

Different organizations use slightly different terms for the same idea. The U.S. General Accounting Office (1997) speaks of "impairments" in one's ability to be fair and just. These impairments can come not only from financial and career interests, but also from values, attitudes, and political views. However phrased, and with appreciation for the nuances of phrasing, the evaluator cannot, this principle makes clear, take sides. This is quite different from reporting findings that may favor the interests of one party or another. Rather, it means conducting the evaluation so that the findings are not slanted beginning, middle, and end by the evaluator's own passions. By this principle, the evaluator must forego balancing perceived inequities with a thumb giving greater weight to the scales of the oppressed.

Considering this reading of Principle C, neither the pro-life nor the pro-choice evaluator should be on the evaluation team. Their political positions seem so deeply held as to be considered an impairment to a fair, just, trustworthy evaluation.

**For Advocacy.** Another principle, however, could be read as permitting and perhaps encouraging advocacy in evaluation. Principle E considers responsibility for the general and public welfare. It explicitly states "evaluators have obligations that encompass the public interest and general good . . . clear threats to the public good should never be ignored in any evaluation. Because the public interest and good are rarely the same as the interests of any particular group . . . evaluators will usually have to go beyond an analysis of particular stakeholder interests when considering the welfare of society as a whole" (American Evaluation Association, 1995, pp. 25–26).

A common language reading of this principle requires evaluators to be ever conscious of the public good and general welfare. But the guidelines do not indicate what view of the general welfare and public good is considered: What is stated in law? By currently elected officials? By majority opinion? By the views of whatever group seems most disenfranchised by whatever indicators? By the evaluator's own perception of social justice? As Rossi (1995), discussing this principle, points out, ". . .what is the public good is the bone of contention among political parties, political ideologies, and even world religions" (p. 57). It seems as though evaluators can select any definition of the public good they choose.

What are the implications of this position for the hypothetical abortion clinics' evaluation? Considering this reading of Principle E, depending on your point of view, either the pro-life or the pro-choice evaluator should serve on the team but not both. Moreover, any evaluators who have not thought through what the common good and general welfare mean on this issue (that is, on abortion) should reach a position as part of their responsibility.

It seems noteworthy that the basis for Principle E is not a belief that evaluators are irremediably unable to be objective, but rather that we serve a higher social good beyond serving those in charge and the proximal and intermediate stakeholders, such as staff and participants of a particular program. To do only the bidding of those paying for the evaluation is seen as making evaluation little more than market research. Although responsible to our clients, whether internal or external, we are equally responsible, in light of this principle, for considering the general good and public welfare.

Exactly what evaluators have to do beyond "considering" is left unstated. Presumably it includes infusing all aspects of the evaluation with the representation of the ultimate stakeholder—the public good as understood by the evaluator—in the same way one would a more proximal stakeholder.

## Common Ground

This brief analysis illustrates what many other evaluators have already noted (see, for example, Rossi, 1995). The principles apparently can be cited in support of neutrality or advocacy in evaluation. It is therefore not to the AEA Guiding Principles as stated that evaluators might look for standards of conduct in specific cases or for a reconciliation, if this is possible, between apparently irreconcilable views.

The ambiguity of the AEA Guiding Principles is consistent with the intentional difference between the general guidance of principles and the operational guidance of standards. Rossi (1995) commented: "The membership of AEA is divided on a number of critical and substantive technical issues. A strongly worded set of standards might easily sunder the weak bonds that bind us together and nullify the compromises that make AEA possible" (p. 56).

The principles developed between 1992 and 1994 were intended as part of continuing discussions on ethical issues. They served us well then, in offering an ecumenical framework for robust discourse on ethics. Seven years later, however, the principles may need refreshing in order to reflect new approaches, such as *emergent realism* (Henry, Julnes, and Mark, 1998), and to guide practice. Indeed, some common ground may be present in the values shared by various perspectives on the ethics of evaluation advocacy and neutrality. That is, by examining possible common denominators in recent commentaries on these issues, we may get back to a sense of how to balance apparently competing principles.

Two striking common denominators are the value placed on fairness and faithfulness to all stakeholders and on respecting deeply the dignity of all stakeholders and their right to be heard. A series of recent articles by leaders in our field, such as Lincoln, House, and Greene, gives a window on contemporary definitions of advocacy in evaluation.

This is Lincoln (Ryan, Greene, Lincoln, Mathison, and Mertens, 1998):

> We operate from profound social commitments which honor all stakeholders groups' views and perspectives, whether or not we happen to agree with those views. . . . We speak of "advocacy" as if it meant we go into an evaluation determined to take sides, and that would mean typically, "against" the program managers, administrators, funders, or other critical individuals. When I talk about advocacy, I don't mean taking sides in that more specific sense. What I mean rather refers to becoming an advocate for pluralism, for many voices to feed into the evaluation. . . . What I am advocating for is less a particular individual or group than a position which insists that all stakeholders be identified and solicited for their constructions of the strengths and weaknesses of the program. [pp. 102, 108]

A similar idea was expressed vividly in her discussion (1990) of the need to "express multiple, socially constructed, and often conflicting realities. The latter we termed fairness, and judgments were made on the achievement of this criterion in much the same way that labor negotiators and mediators determine fairness in bargaining sessions" (p. 72).

This is House and Howe (1998):

> We think the framework [of a Chelimsky study] must be something like this: Include conflicting values and stakeholder groups in the study. Make sure all major views are sufficiently included and represented. Bring conflicting views together so there can be deliberation and dialogue about them among the relevant parties. Make sure there is sufficient room for dialogue to resolve conflicting claims, but also to help the policy makers and media resolve these claims by sorting through the good and bad information. . . . Is this advocacy on the part of the evaluators? We would say no, even though their work is heavily value laden and incorporates judgment. It is not advocacy, such as taking [one side or the other] at the beginning of the study and championing only one side or another. . . . We suggest three criteria for evaluations to be properly balanced. . . .

First the study should be inclusive so as to represent all relevant views, interests, values and stakeholders. . . . Second, there should be sufficient dialogue with the relevant groups so that the views are properly and authentically represented. . . . Third, there should be sufficient deliberation to arrive at proper findings. [pp. 234–245]

This is Greene (Ryan, et al., 1998):

Except in unusual circumstances, I do not believe that evaluators should advocate for the program being evaluated. Such advocacy compromises the perceived credibility and thus the persuasiveness of the evaluative claims . . . what evaluators should . . . advocate for is their own value commitment. . . . In participatory evaluation, this value commitment is to democratic pluralism, to broadening the policy conversation to include all legitimate perspectives and voices, and to full and fair stakeholder participation in policy and program decision making . . . the participatory evaluator needs to get in close to the program. . . . But this closeness should not be misconstrued as program partisanship. That is, participatory evaluators do advocate, not for a particular program, but rather for an open, inclusive, engaged conversation among stakeholders about the merit and worth of *their* program . . . of fairly and fully representing all legitimate interests and concerns in an evaluation. [pp. 109, 111]

## Reframing the Discussion

Neutral: A person or group not taking part in a controversy; unaligned with one side or another in a controversy; of no particular kind or characteristic; indefinite
Impartial: Fair, just

With these definitions (Webster's, 1994), a shared theme among the evaluators cited here is impartiality—the sense of fairness and justice. Neutrality, which might initially seem similar, is too passive, connoting a sort of withdrawal from the storms and complexities of the world. Passivity does not seem to me either characteristic of, or common ground for, our field. This review, then, suggests

- Diverse evaluators *agree* that the evaluator should not be an advocate (or presumably, an adversary) of a specific program in the sense of taking sides, of a preconceived position of support (or destruction).
- There is *agreement* that the evaluator should be an advocate for making sure that as many relevant cards as possible get laid on the table, face up, with the values (worth, merit) showing.
- There is *agreement* that the evaluator must be aware of how less powerful voices or unpopular views, positions, information can get silenced and make special efforts to ensure that these voices (data, view, information) get heard.

Therefore, it may be helpful to reframe the discussions in terms of impartiality or fairness. No evaluation approach of which I know would countenance (1) *deliberately* ignoring program theories leading to different expectations about what should be studied or measured, or what results to look for, (2) *deliberately* selecting measures or questions to favor one side over another, (3) *deliberately* misquoting what an interviewee said, (4) *deliberately* creating data out of the whole cloth to prove a point, (5) *deliberately* going from the reams of raw data to conclusions by a sneaky path supporting one side over another, (6) *deliberately* failing to listen to the views of all parties with conflicting perspectives, (7) *deliberately* suppressing information that did not support the evaluator's own values or the results the evaluator wished to obtain, (8) *deliberately* using words that cumulatively skew the report to one side or the other, or (9) *deliberately* presenting complex, nuanced findings in a simplistic way to favor one position over another (Datta, 1997). Perhaps these points are a start toward expressing standards in this area with which many evaluators could agree.

This is not to say that we may not inadvertently in practice—through methodological limitations, ignorance of how our own views and language create subtle biases, or failure to use strategies for achieving fair and faithful evaluations—do all of the above or more. Rather, it is to say that as I read recent efforts to articulate what we mean, I find that we seek balance and want fairness, like a mighty river, to pour down.

## QED? No, Dilemmas Will Remain in Application to Practice

Principles are not standards on how to be fair and just in practice. What principles mean in practice is likely to require continued reexamination and reinterpretation as experience grows, evaluation theories develop, and new technologies arise. For example, to some evaluators, such as Greene and Mertens, closeness and inclusion are essential. The evaluator models, by how the evaluation itself is done, ideals of empowerment, demarginalization of the disenfranchised and oppressed, and in so doing reaps many evaluation benefits such as greater authenticity, better balance, greater fairness, "natural" evaluation utilization. Since truth lies in the eye of the beholder, one logically gets as many beholders as possible.

To others, such as Scriven (1997), opinions and self-interest lie in the eye of the involved stakeholders, albeit experienced by them as truth. Closeness is to be avoided, risking as it does co-option and bias. Also to be avoided is being impartial on an issue during working hours but an adversary or advocate on the same issue when the meter isn't running. Inclusion of relevant, but unpopular or silenced views, to such evaluators is as crucial to evaluation as it is to those encouraging closeness. The techniques for achieving such inclusion are not seen as requiring sitting around a table, as it were, with the evaluator as moderator when decisions are made about design, measures, analyses, and reports. Rather, the techniques include using extant data and relying on per-formance data rather than staff interviews, and where such interviews are essential, being sure they involve prestructuring based on other data and are conducted by well-trained, well-supervised interviewers. Other approaches include goal-free methods, heavy interviewing with consumers and other stakeholders, and in all of this, applying quality control procedures such as audiotape backups. Parenthetically, a fine example of an evaluation using such approaches in a responsive evaluation framework is now available (Stake, Davis, and Guynn, 1997).

Chelimsky (1997) is pragmatic about methods for achieving inclusive-ness. Though considerably less daunted than Scriven about being captured, subdued, or co-opted by sitting down with stakeholders, she would be highly on her guard against efforts to coerce evaluators or otherwise place them in an advocacy or adversary position. (For example, being set up as a Congressional pit-bull chomping on a possibly effective but out-of-favor pro-gram such as WIC would be as threatening to the GAO's independence and credibility as being cast as a shill for a possibly ineffective but popular pro-gram such as chemical warfare.)

Are Greene and Mertens talking about different types of programs than Scriven and Chelimsky, and thus the apparent disagreements are a case of "It depends"? Evaluators vary in the ease of public access to evaluations they have completed, or in how closely anchored their discussions of advocacy and neu-trality are in specific work. It seems likely that positions recommending close-ness and inclusiveness are more feasible with fairly small-scale evaluations, perhaps on local or state levels. For example, one could bring out all stake-holders' voices fairly in a small program, such as a local Hospice Center, an individual school, or even a county-wide recycling program.

In contrast, although it is easy to envision inclusiveness in a national eval-uation, it is more difficult to imagine one-on-one closeness. As an example, the first issue of the new Head Start journal aimed at promoting researcher-evaluator and practitioner dialogue focuses on stakeholder collaboration and participation, but includes examples only from small studies, not the many national evaluations. However, some federal agencies now are writing Requests for Proposals (RFPs) consistent with empowerment and participatory views (such as the Bureau of Indian Affairs), so in the future, we may be able to see more empirically the transportability of the inclusive, close, participatory approach.

Personally, I would like to read, in full, an evaluation someone has com-pleted (several, if possible) as a way of seeing what difference the principles make in practice and where, if any place, "it depends." We might be somewhat farther along if such evaluations were easily available as companion pieces to the more theoretical articles. House (1995) wisely wrote, "It is difficult to write intelligently about ethics and values. One reason is that ethical problems are manifested only in particular concrete cases and endorsement of general prin-ciples sometimes seems platitudinous or irrelevant. Ethical concerns become interesting only in conflicted cases" (p. 27). The AEA conference sessions on ethical questions and how various evaluators would address them (Morris, 1997; Nelkin, 1995) as well as the "Ethical Challenges" series in the *American Journal of Evaluation* represent exceptionally valuable means to this good end, as are reports such as Bell (1997) and Bickman (1996).

In a Great State, the legislature decides to go with charter schools and vouchers, so parents can send their child to the school of their choice: public, private, parochial. The stated intents are to improve student learning, improve the quality of all education, improve public confidence in and support of education, and equalize the playing field by ethnicity and family income in opportunities to learn. An evaluation team is asked to judge the merit, worth, and value of the program as implemented in achieving the benefits sought. One member of the team is strongly pro-choice, believing that social justice and equity require giving charter schools and vouchers a chance. Another member of the team is strongly anti-choice, believing that the best way to improve public education is to improve public education and that the school choice program will drain brains and money from already beleaguered public schools.

Should either of these evaluators participate in the study? My answer is that in a study such as this and the abortion clinic scenario that began this chapter, one way—but not the only way—of ensuring balance, fairness, and a less corruptible evaluation is that the team include *both* evaluators (see also Bell, 1997; Datta, 1997).

The team as a whole should make clear to the school board and all stakeholders their diversity of beliefs, how their differences may affect and improve the evaluation, and what else they will do to be in compliance with Principle C (revised): Evaluators should be impartial, taking steps to promote the fairness, balance and justice of the entire evaluation process.

## References

American Evaluation Association, Task Force on Guiding Principles for Evaluators. "Guiding Principles for Evaluators." In W. R. Shadish, D. L. Newman, M. A. Scheirer, and C. Wye (eds.), *Guiding Principles for Evaluators.* New Directions for Program Evaluation, no. 66. San Francisco: Jossey-Bass, 1995.

Bell, S. "Crafting a Non-Partisan Evaluation in a Partisan World: The Urban Institute New Federalism Evaluation." Paper presented at the American Evaluation Association Conference, San Diego, November 1997.

Bickman, L. "Implications of the Fort Bragg Evaluation." *Evaluation Practice,* 1996, *17,* 57–74.

Chelimsky, E. "The Political Environment of Evaluation and What It Means for the Development of the Field." In E. Chelimsky and W. Shadish (eds.). *Evaluation for the 21st Century: A Handbook.* Thousand Oaks, Calif.: Sage, 1997.

Cook, T. D. "Lessons Learned in Evaluation Over the Past 25 Years." In E. Chelimsky and W. R. Shadish (eds.), *Evaluation for the 21st Century: A Handbook.* Thousand Oaks, Calif.: Sage, 1997.

Datta, L. "Crafting Non-partisan Evaluations in a Partisan World." Paper presented at the American Evaluation Association Conference, San Diego, November 1997.

Fetterman, D. "Empowerment Evaluation and Accreditation in Higher Education." In E. Chelimsky and W. R. Shadish (eds.) *Evaluation for the 21st Century: A Handbook.* Thousand Oaks, Calif.: Sage, 1997.

Greene, J. C. "Evaluation as Advocacy." *Evaluation Practice,* 1995, *18,* 25–36.

Henry, G. T., Julnes, G., and Mark, M. M. (eds.). *Realist Evaluation: An Emerging Theory in Support of Practice.* New Directions for Evaluation, no. 78. San Francisco: Jossey-Bass, 1998.

House, E. R., and Howe, K. R. "The Issue of Advocacy in Evaluations." *American Journal of Evaluation.* 1998, *19,* 233–236.

House, E. R. "Principled Evaluation: A Critique of the AEA Guiding Principles." In W. R. Shadish, D. L. Newman, M. A. Scheirer, and C. Wye (eds.), *New Directions for Evaluation,* 66. San Francisco: Jossey-Bass, 1995.

Lincoln, Y. "The Making of a Constructivist: A Remembrance of Transformations Past." In E. Guba, *The Paradigm Dialog.* Thousand Oaks, Calif.: Sage, 1990.

Mertens, D. "Identifying and Respecting Differences Among Participants in Evaluation Studies." In W. R. Shadish, D. Newman, M. A. Scheirer, and C. Wye (eds.), *Guiding Principles for Evaluators.* New Directions for Program Evaluation, no. 66. San Francisco: Jossey-Bass, 1995.

Morris, M. (Chair). "What's an Evaluator to Do? Confronting Ethical Dilemmas in Practice." Session presented at the American Evaluation Association Conference, San Diego, November 1997.

Nelkin, V. S. (Chair). "Ethical Dilemmas in Evaluation." Session presented at the American Evaluation Association Conference, Vancouver, B.C., November 1995.

Rossi, P.H. "Doing Good and Getting It Right." In W. R. Shadish, D. Newman, M .A. Scheirer, and C. Wye (eds.), *Guiding Principles for Evaluators.* New Directions for Program Evaluation, no. 66. San Francisco: Jossey-Bass, 1995.

Ryan, K., Greene, J., Lincoln, Y., Mathison, S., and Mertens, D. M. "Advantages and Disadvantages of Using Inclusive Evaluation Approaches in Evaluation Practice." *American Journal of Evaluation,* 1998, *19,* 101–122.

Scriven, M. "Truth and Objectivity in Evaluation." In E. Chelimsky and W. Shadish (eds.), *Evaluation for the 21st Century: A Handbook.* Thousand Oaks, Calif.: Sage, 1997.

Stake, R.E., Davis, R., and Guynn, S. *Evaluation of Reader Focused Writing for the Veterans Benefits Administration.* Champaign, Illinois: CIRCE at the University of Illinois, 1997.

United States General Accounting Office. *Auditing Standards.* Washington, D.C.: Author, 1997.

*Webster's Encyclopedic Unabridged Dictionary of the English Language.* New York: Gramercy Books, 1994.

*LOIS-ELLIN DATTA, president of Datta Analysis, is a past president of the Evaluation Research Society and recipient of the Alva and Gunnar Myrdal Award for Evaluation in Government Service and of the Robert Ingel Award for Extraordinary Service to the American Evaluation Association. She has been director of research and evaluation for Project Head Start and the Children's Bureau; director for teaching, learning, and assessment at the National Institute of Education; and Director for Program Evaluation in the Human Services Area at the U.S. Government Accounting Office.*

*There has been little discussion in evaluation literature in the United States of ethical issues in conducting evaluation in international settings. Although many of the same ethical issues arise wherever the evaluation is conducted, two sets of ethical issues that are particularly important in developing countries concern how stakeholders should be involved and to what extent the evaluator should respect local customs and values.*

# Ethical Issues in Conducting Evaluation in International Settings

*Michael Bamberger*

This chapter reviews some of the ethical issues identified in evaluations in the United States and considers the similarities and differences in application of these issues in developing countries. It also identifies a number of ethical issues arising in international evaluations that are less common in U.S. domestic evaluations. These concern the role of international agencies in financing, promoting, and conducting evaluation in developing countries and how the political, economic, and cultural characteristics of developing countries affect evaluation practice. We refer frequently to the Joint Committee's *Program Evaluation Standards* and the American Evaluation Association's (AEA) "Guiding Principles for Evaluation" as illustrations of how U.S. evaluators have approached issues relating to professional evaluation standards and to show how these approaches have been viewed from the perspective of developing countries.

## Ethical Issues in International Evaluation

This chapter is concerned primarily with evaluations in developing countries that are conducted by, or sponsored by, multilateral development agencies (World Bank, UNICEF, InterAmerican Development Bank, for example), bilateral development agencies (USAID, CIDA), international nongovernmental organizations (NGOs) (OXFAM, CARE, World Vision), and North American or European-based research institutes (universities). Evaluations that are conducted by national governments, universities, or NGOs without international sponsorship are not directly addressed, though the discussion may have implications for these evaluations.

Almost all international development agencies (whether multilateral, bilateral, or NGO) require that the projects or programs they sponsor be evaluated. In some cases, these agencies will conduct the evaluations themselves or will commission them through international and local consultants, whereas in other cases they will require that the borrower or grantee conduct the evaluation. Many of these development agencies are also concerned with strengthening evaluation capacity in developing countries through training, study tours, provision of international experts, or financial support.

These international development agencies provide the major source of funding and the main impetus for program evaluation in many developing countries. They have, in fact, often been responsible for introducing the concept of program evaluation to these countries. There are probably still a considerable number of countries in which these agencies are the *only* sponsors of systematic program evaluation. Although federal and state agencies are among the main funders of evaluations in the United States and clearly have a major influence on the evaluation agenda and evaluation practice, it is likely that international development agencies, given their very broad development roles, have an even greater influence on international evaluation and must address an even wider range of ethical issues in their program evaluations and evaluation capacity-building activities.

A review of the *Program Evaluation Standards* and the *Guiding Principles for Evaluators*, both of which are discussed in other chapters, identifies five sets of ethical issues of particular importance in the international evaluation context:

1.  Respect for multiculturalism and diversity. This involves respect for different cultural values, particularly with respect to individuals and groups who are politically and culturally vulnerable.
2.  Protecting the legitimate concerns of clients and stakeholders. Many international evaluations involve a delicate balancing act between the concerns of clients and the often conflicting interests of a wide variety of stakeholders.
3.  Ensuring the cultural appropriateness of the evaluation approach. A frequently heard criticism is that international evaluators seek uncritically to introduce methods used in the United States without assessing their cultural and methodological appropriateness in different international contexts.
4.  Dissemination of information on evaluation methods, findings, and proposed actions. In many international settings, both clients and stakeholders may be unfamiliar with the proposed methodologies and even with the concept of evaluation. Evaluation can be seen by many groups as a potential threat, so the evaluator has an ethical responsibility to ensure that all affected groups understand the potential risks and benefits of the evaluations.
5.  Meeting the needs of different stakeholders and the general public (utility). International evaluations frequently respond to the needs of the

donor agency. An ethical challenge is to ensure that the evaluation process seeks to develop national evaluation capacity and also responds to the information needs of the host country.

I have selected two ethical dilemmas, which reflect many of the issues underlying all of these challenges, for discussion in the remainder of this chapter: (1) To what extent should the evaluator respect local customs and values? (2) How should we involve stakeholders in international settings?

## To What Extent Should the Evaluator Respect Local Customs and Values?

Issues of multiculturalism and diversity are now widely discussed in the U.S. evaluation literature (Mertens, 1995; Gill, 1998). Guiding Principle D.5 concerns identifying and respecting differences among participants in all phases of the evaluation. However, Mertens and others argue that mainstream evaluations frequently ignore or inadequately address issues such as the handicapped, ethnicity, and gender. Given the lack of understanding of these issues even within the relatively sophisticated U.S. evaluation community, it is not surprising that multiculturalism and diversity offer particularly difficult ethical challenges in the international evaluation arena.

A recent discussion among evaluators from outside the United States on the AEA Guiding Principles (Hendricks and Conner, 1995) was useful in illustrating some of the difficulties in transferring U.S. evaluation paradigms to other cultural contexts. In many developing countries, they observed, evaluation is a recent phenomenon. In other countries, political developments have a great deal of influence on evaluation. Many other cultural differences that influence how evaluation is conducted are noted by these evaluators.

Although the AEA Guiding Principles, as noted, emphasize the need to respect differences in culture, carrying out this principle can be difficult in developing countries. International researchers and evaluators are frequently criticized for ignoring or showing a lack of respect for local culture. For example, some gender research is criticized for introducing concepts of political and economic empowerment in a way that ignores cultural values concerning marriage and religion. Hence, advocacy for girls' education as a form of economic and political empowerment overlooks cultural values that view such education as threatening the stability of the family. Preparatory research might have shown that strong support for girls' education could have been obtained by linking it to improvements in the economic welfare of the household—a value that is widely accepted.

Studies on community participation and political development may introduce Western models of political pluralism and democracy that are inappropriate in other cultures. For example, the concept of stakeholder is seen in some cultures as promoting conflict and challenging the traditional goal of consensus building. Cultural values are also apparent in our operational definitions.

Poverty assessments often use quantitative measures of poverty that are based on income and calorie consumption but that ignore concepts such as vulnerability and isolation, which may be better understood by members of the communities being studied. Finally, female genital mutilation (FGM) is a very controversial area in which Western researchers are frequently criticized for trivializing the social customs surrounding this practice. However, many would argue that the defense of basic human rights overrides the need to respect cultural values.

**Evaluating the Gender Dimensions of Development.** A challenge in international evaluation is to give voice to women and other vulnerable groups (Mertens, 1995). In many countries, gender issues do not have a high priority. There is often resistance to the intervention of international agencies in what are considered religious or culturally sensitive areas. How should international evaluators ethically address these issues? Actions in this area can conflict with the goal of respecting local customs. When evaluators require that women participate with men in community meetings or in focus groups, they may be criticized for violating local values. It is, however, important to avoid a unidimensional focus on gender (Pollard, 1992). The status of women is affected by the interactions among gender, class, and ethnicity, and it is ethically important for the evaluation to recognize women's diversity by adopting a multidimensional focus. Not all women are disadvantaged and in need of special assistance. For example, in many cultures, middle-class women may have much greater economic and political freedom than poor men.

Though gender issues are regularly addressed in sectors such as health and education, gender is largely ignored in the "hard" investment sectors such as transport, energy, and large-scale water supply and sanitation projects. There is growing, but often not very well documented, evidence that gender-neutral investment projects either benefit women less than men, or can even have negative consequences for some groups of women (Bamberger and Lebo, 1999). For example, in many rural areas of Africa, women headload up to 70 percent of water, fuel, and agricultural produce; yet rural transport projects focus more on motorized transport, which benefits men more than women (Barwell, 1996).

**Ethical Issues in the Use of Western Experimental Designs.** Scientific evaluation methods raise several ethical questions. First, evaluators frequently consider that most impact evaluations should seek to approximate an experimental design that uses, where possible, a randomized design or the closest practical approximation. However, such designs raise a number of important ethical issues. First, the design can create false expectations. The author has had the experience in several countries of being approached by people requesting to be included in the control group so that they will be eligible for the next phase of the (housing, health, or similar) project. Second, there have been numerous criticisms of medical research in which the control group is denied access to treatment for AIDS, immunization, or programs for pregnant women ("CDC Overseas Research . . .," 1998). Other questions arise when the treatment being tested is too expensive to be made generally available to the population being tested.

## How Should We Involve Stakeholders in International Settings?

Participatory evaluation is now widely advocated as a way to empower intended beneficiaries and to ensure that evaluations and the programs they support are based on an understanding of the values and culture of the affected populations. Participatory approaches broaden the political dialogue by giving voice to a wider range of interests, a function that is compatible with Guiding Principle D.5. But broadening the political dialogue in developing countries can create tensions and conflicts that may have negative repercussions for groups who are seen as challenging the status quo. For example, men may react violently when wives or children express their views; village elders and local political leaders may apply sanctions against those who question their authority; and government officials may limit services in the face of criticism. Although tension and conflict are often an inevitable part of political empowerment, outsiders must first fully examine the potential consequences of challenging the status quo and must ensure that the groups with whom they are working are fully aware of the consequences of their actions. This is a particularly strong ethical requirement for outsiders, who may naively encourage involvement without being fully aware of the risks of violence, severe economic sanctions, or even, in extreme cases, imprisonment or death to at-risk stakeholders.

Second, outside evaluators must seek to adapt their participatory approaches to traditional patterns of discussion, organization, and conflict resolution. Attempts to force men and women to meet together to discuss problems may not be appropriate or effective in some contexts. Outsiders must ensure that ideological concerns for gender equality or broadened political participation do not lead them to impose forms of organization that may not work in a particular context.

Many cultures appear to outsiders to permit very little debate or participation as meetings are conducted in a very formal way with everyone seeming to agree with the local leadership. This consensus can be very misleading, however. Many cultures place a high value on consensus building and the avoidance of conflict. In the kampungs of Indonesia, for example, local community leaders meet individually with families and often engage in very lively debates until the concerns of each family have been discussed. However, conflicts will normally be resolved and deals will have been made during these face-to-face discussions. It is expected that public meetings will reflect consensus. Attempts by outsiders to promote discussion during community meetings would be strongly resisted.

**Respecting the Value of Respondent's Time.** Evaluation can be burdensome and disrespectful of the respondent. Many evaluations make very heavy demands on the time of respondents, particularly in the poorest sectors of society. Respondents may be asked to spend several hours responding to surveys and may be expected to take time off from work to be available for the interviewer. Many participatory methods make a value of encouraging communities to be actively involved in the evaluation process, often through spending considerable time in group meetings and Participatory Rural Appraisal (PRA) activities. Typically, the researchers are of a higher status than most of the people they are studying and often show very little consideration for sacrifices that the respondents must make. Is payment to respondents in recognition of their time and inconvenience appropriate? Many researchers argue that payment might bias the responses (in addition to increasing the cost of the study). Very often, respect for the respondent is not a central concern in this discussion.

**The Role of the Evaluator and Multiple Stakeholders.** In many countries evaluations of development programs are largely funded by one or more international agencies. These agencies frequently initiate the idea of conducting the evaluation and define the objectives, the methodology, and how the evaluation findings should be disseminated. The dominance of the funding agency raises ethical questions concerning who owns the evaluation and to what extent agencies in the host country own, or have control over, how the evaluation is designed and used. There are clearly ethical issues to be addressed at the level of individual evaluations and at the level of national development.

The evaluator faces ethical dilemmas in balancing the desires of the funding agency with those of other stakeholders. International evaluators frequently have to respond to the needs both of donor agencies and the national agencies that implement the projects. Each agency has different requirements, some of which may conflict. For example, donor agencies may wish to conduct quantitative economic analysis whereas local agencies may wish to conduct more qualitative studies to assess the social impacts of the programs. Or the opposite may be true. Donors also can create ethical conflicts for the evaluator by pressing them for information unrelated to the evaluation. Donors often look upon the evaluator as one of their key sources of information about the organization. Their push for information creates conflicting loyalties for the evaluator and distrust between the evaluator and national agencies.

These agencies may be under pressure to show positive results of programs or to justify requests for larger budgets. Evaluators may be pressured not to report on some less satisfactory aspects of the program. Frequently, national planning and implementing agencies have limited professional resources and may consequently make significant demands on the time of the evaluators to carry out non-evaluation activities—often to the frustration of the donor agencies who have hired the evaluators.

An important issue often concerns the language in which reports are published. Donors will often require that reports be published in English (or another language of the donor country). The reports may therefore be inaccessible to stakeholder groups such as local government agencies, community organizations, and women's groups who are not fluent in these official languages. Many of the poorest and most vulnerable groups are, then, effectively excluded from access to the evaluation findings.

Other conflicts can occur because different stakeholders may have different expectations concerning the role of the evaluator. Many evaluators, including nationals, have been trained in Western universities and seek to apply the standards of professional rigor they have learned in these countries. This desire for statistical rigor may be compounded by the evaluator's desire to impress their academic colleagues, thus making their reports inaccessible to many, nonresearch-oriented audiences. Conversely, in many cultures, loyalty to the organization overrides objectivity and rigor; researchers may thus find themselves under pressure to withhold or distort findings.

Finally, many developing countries are not accustomed to open criticism that evaluations can entail. The survival of projects, funding agencies, and evaluators can be seriously threatened by negative or questioning evaluations (Hendricks and Conner, 1995). Consequently, many evaluators will be reluctant to be too critical of the organizations.

**The Need for Professional Reporting Standards for Participatory and Other Qualitative Evaluations.** The reader of an international evaluation based on quantitative survey methods will expect to find detailed documentation on the research hypotheses, sample design, data analysis, and usually a copy of the survey instrument. However, whereas PRA and other participatory methods do have guidelines for documenting their methodology, many participatory evaluation practitioners in developing countries do not feel obliged to provide this documentation. For example, many participatory evaluations that draw most of their findings from group discussions and other group activities provide very little information on how group participants were selected, exactly what questions were asked, or the procedures used to ensure that the views of all participants were taken into consideration.

Professional reporting standards for participatory evaluations are particularly important in many developing contexts for several reasons. First, local researchers and project managers may not have access to the professional expertise to evaluate the research designs and may take findings on trust to a greater extent than might be the case in the United States. Second, given limited resources for evaluation studies in developing countries, the findings and recommendations of individual studies may have a greater impact on policy and project design decisions than would usually be the case in the United States. This raises important ethical as well as methodological issues, because the purpose of many of these studies is to identify community priorities or to evaluate the impacts of development projects on vulnerable population groups. Policy makers and planners need this information to ensure that the views expressed, and the priorities identified, do in fact represent the views of all sectors of the community and not only those of a small, vocal elite (or even worse the views of the researcher). It is therefore important to develop, and enforce, professionally acceptable reporting standards for participatory and qualitative evaluation research.

## Conclusion

There has been relatively little formal discussion of ethical issues in international evaluation. The *Program Evaluation Standards* and the *Guiding Principles for Evaluators* both provide useful starting points for the identification of the main ethical issues to be addressed in the international evaluation arena. However, both of these reports were designed for U.S. domestic evaluators and not all of the principles can be directly translated to the context of developing countries. It is necessary to understand the effects of local social, economic, and cultural contexts on how evaluation is approached. It is particularly important to take into account the fact that most evaluations of development programs are promoted, and often implemented and even disseminated, by international development agencies. There is a concern that the questions being asked and the methods used often reflect more the concerns of the donor agency, and the international evaluation consultants, than those of the host country.

Two sets of ethical issues were discussed: (1) respecting local customs and values, and (2) involving stakeholders in international settings. Extensive experience on the ethical dimensions of each of these issues can be found in the U.S. evaluation literature, but much of this experience has not yet been translated into the international arena. U.S. domestic evaluators and their international development evaluation colleagues would both benefit from a greater exchange of experiences and approaches to these issues.

## References

Bamberger, M., and Lebo, J. "Gender and Transport: A Rationale for Action." *PREM Notes,* no. 14. Poverty Reduction and Economic Management Department. Washington, D.C.: The World Bank, 1999.

Barwell, I. *Transport and the Village.* World Bank Discussion Paper No. 344, Washington, D.C.: World Bank, 1996.

"CDC Overseas Research Doesn't Include Ethics Agreement." *Cleveland Plain Dealer,* Nov. 9, 1998.

Gill, C. "Invisible Ubiquity: The Surprising Relevance of Disability Issues in Evaluation." Paper presented at the American Evaluation Association Conference, Chicago, Nov. 5, 1998.

Hendricks, M., and Connor, R. "International Perspectives on the Guiding Principles." In W. Shadish, D. Newman, M. A. Scheirer, and C. Wye. (eds.), *Guiding Principles for Evaluation.* New Directions for Program Evaluation, no. 66. San Francisco: Jossey-Bass, 1995.

Mertens, D. "Identifying and Respecting Differences Among Participants in Evaluation Studies." In W. Shadish, D. Newman, M. A. Scheirer, and C. Wye. (eds.), *Guiding Principles for Evaluation.* New Directions for Program Evaluation, no. 66. San Francisco: Jossey-Bass, 1995.

Pollard, D. S. "Towards a Pluralistic Perspective on Equity." *Women's Education Equity Act Publishing Center Digest,* 1992, 7, 1–2.

*MICHAEL BAMBERGER has been involved in international program evaluation for the past thirty years. He was adviser on monitoring and evaluation to the Urban Department of the World Bank for several years and has conducted evaluations in Africa, Asia, Latin America, and the Middle East. He currently works in the Gender and Development Group in the Poverty Reduction and Economic Management Department of the World Bank.*

# INDEX

AAA. *See* American Anthropology Association
ABA. *See* American Bar Association
Academic proof, versus action proof, 30
Action proof, versus academic proof, 30
Adams, K. A., 26, 30
Advocacy. *See* Evaluation advocacy/ neutrality
AEA. *See* American Evaluation Association
AEA Guiding Principles. *See Guiding Principles for Evaluators* (AEA)
AERA. *See* American Educational Research Association
AICPA. *See* American Institute of Certified Public Accountants
Albrecht, W. S., 10, 11
Altschuld, J. W., 72, 73
AMA. *See* American Medical Association
American Anthropology Association (AAA), 7, 12
American Bar Association (ABA), 11
American Educational Research Association (AERA), 7, 12, 70
American Evaluation Association (AEA), 1, 6–13, 15, 36, 40–41, 47–48, 57–58, 62, 77–78, 82, 87
American Institute of Certified Public Accountants (AICPA), 9–13
*American Journal of Evaluation, The,* 13, 87
American Medical Association (AMA), 11
American Psychological Association (APA), 7, 9, 11–12, 49, 51, 70
American Society for Public Administration (ASPA), 9, 12
Annie E. Casey Foundation, 36
APA. *See* American Psychological Association
ASPA Code of Ethics, 12
Aspen Institute (Roundtable on Comprehensive Community Initiatives for Children and Families), 36
Australasian Evaluation Society, 6
Ayers, T. S., 15, 47

Bamberger, M., 3, 89, 92
Barwell, I., 92
Bayles, M. D., 8–9, 10

Bell, S., 87
*Belmont Report,* 7
Bentham, J., 68
Bickman, L., 20, 87
Big science, 38
Biglan, A., 20
Bloom, G. A., 57
Bonnet, D. G., 17, 22
Brandon, P. R., 23
Brown, R, D., 2, 16, 18–19, 22, 57–58, 62, 69, 71–73

Campbell, B., 3, 47
Campbell, D., 5
Campbell, D. T., 52
Canada, 6
Caracelli, V., 57–58
"CDC Overseas Research Doesn't Include Ethics Agreement" (*Cleveland Plain Dealer*) 92
Censorship, 53–54
Chelimsky, E., 72, 79, 83–84
Chicago Community Trust, 36
Code of Federal Regulations, 48–49
Code of Professional Conduct (AICPA), 13
Coercion, 48
Cohn, R., 16–19, 22–23, 26, 63, 73
Communities: and comprehensive community initiative, 36; foundation manager's partnership with, 36; and internal-external evaluators, 25, 27–29; relationship of grant-maker to, 37–39
Connecticut Center for School Change, 35–36
Conner, R., 91, 95
Consensus, and enforcement mechanisms, 12
Consent, informed, 47, 48
Consulting professionals, versus scholarly professionals, 8–9
Context-confirmatory approach, 53
Cook, T. D., 54, 79
Cost-benefit analysis, 48–49
Cousins, J. B., 57, 63–64
Covert, R. W., 6–7
Crago, M., 20
Cross-boundary communications, 42

for evaluators, 43–44; role of, within a changing evaluation environment, 39–40; and shifting paradigm of evaluation, 35–37

Garberg, R., 21
Gender issues, 92
Gensheimer, L. K., 15, 47
Gill, C., 91
Gonda, G., 26
Gotkin, V., 20
Government, 1, 77
Government Accounting Office, 6
Government Performance and Results Act (GPRA), 1
Greene, J. C., 80, 83–86
Greene, J. G., 57
Greenwood, D. J., 63
Guba, E. G., 57, 69
*Guiding Principles for Evaluators* (AEA), 1–2, 6–8, 10, 13, 15, 20, 22–23, 25, 36–37, 41, 47–48, 50, 53, 58, 61–62, 64, 70, 78, 81–82, 87, 89–91, 93, 96
Guynn, S., 86

Hammes, R. R., 20
Hamner, K., 20
Hartford Foundation for Public Giving, 36
Hartwell, S. W., 21
Harvard University School of Health, 36, 41
Hawes, J. A., 20
Heflinger, C. A., 20
Hendricks, M., 32, 91, 95
Henry, G. T., 51–53, 83
Heron, J., 61
Honea, G. E., 16–17, 18
Horsch, K., 36, 41
House, E. R., 6–8, 10–12, 26, 32, 57, 64, 69, 83–84, 86–87
Howe, K. R., 57, 64, 83–84
Hume, D., 68

Inclusiveness, 85–87
Informed consent, 47, 48
Institutional review boards, 54
Internal controls, 12
Internal-external evaluator, 26–32
International settings: ethical issues in, 89–91; and evaluator respect for local customs and values, 91–93; fairness and justice in, 85–87; and gender dimensions of development, 92; and

involvement of stakeholders, 93; and multiple stakeholders, 94–95; and need for professional reporting standards, 95; and respect for value of respondent's time, 93–94; and use of Western experimental designs, 92–93
Interviews, 86
*It's Up to You* (AICPA), 13

Jekel, J. F., 21
Johnson, P. L., 49
Joint Committee on Standards for Educational Evaluation, 5–8, 13, 15, 47–48, 57, 62
Joint Committee Standards. *See Standards for Evaluations of Educational Programs, Projects, and Materials* (Joint Committee on Standards for Educational Evaluation)
Jones, E. G., 19
Julnes, G., 51–53, 83

Kant, I., 68
Kirkhart, K., 26
Kitchner, K. S., 69

Lam, J. A., 21
Lebo, J., 92
Levin, M., 63
Lincoln, Y. S., 57, 69, 79–80, 83
Lipsey, M. W., 54
Littell, L., 26
Lobosco, A. F., 73
Local customs and values, 91–93
Lord, G. L., 15, 21
Love, A. J., 26
Lueptow, L., 20

Mabry, L., 15, 57
Macarthur Foundation, 36
Manpower Demonstration Research Corporation, 38
Mariner, W. K., 48–49, 51
Mark, M. M., 3, 47, 51–53, 83
Master, L. R., 20
Mathison, S., 2, 16, 25–26, 28, 31–32, 71–72, 83
McKillip, J., 21
McTaggart, R., 61
Mercier, C., 23
Mertens, D. M., 59, 63–64, 69, 73, 80, 83, 85–86, 91, 92
Merton, V., 50

# Back Issue/Subscription Order Form

Copy or detach and send to:
**Jossey-Bass Inc., Publishers, 350 Sansome Street, San Francisco, CA 94104-1342**

Call or fax toll free!
**Phone 888-378-2537 6AM-5PM PST; Fax 800-605-2665**

Back issues:     Please send me the following issues at $23 each.
(Important: please include series initials and issue number, such as EV90.)

EV _____

_____

_____

$ _____ Total for single issues

$ _____ Shipping charges (for single issues *only;* subscriptions are exempt from shipping charges): Up to $30, add $5$^{50}$ • $30$^{01}$–$50, add $6$^{50}$ $50$^{01}$–$75, add $7$^{50}$ • $75$^{01}$–$100, add $9 • $100$^{01}$–$150, add $10 Over $150, call for shipping charge.

Subscriptions     Please ❏ start    ❏ renew my subscription to *New Directions for Evaluation* for the year 19___ at the following rate:

❏ Individual $65          ❏ Institutional $115
**NOTE:** Subscriptions are quarterly, and are for the calendar year only. Subscriptions begin with the spring issue of the year indicated above. For shipping outside the U.S., please add $25.

$ _____ Total single issues and subscriptions (CA, IN, NJ, NY, and DC residents, add sales tax for single issues. NY and DC residents must include shipping charges when calculating sales tax. NY and Canadian residents only, add sales tax for subscriptions.)

❏ Payment enclosed (U.S. check or money order only)

❏ VISA, MC, AmEx, Discover Card #_____ Exp. date_____

Signature _____ Day phone _____

❏ Bill me (U.S. institutional orders only. Purchase order required.)

Purchase order #_____

Name _____

Address _____

_____

_____

Phone_____ E-mail _____

For more information about Jossey-Bass Publishers, visit our Web site at:
www.josseybass.com          **PRIORITY CODE = ND1**

OTHER TITLES AVAILABLE IN THE
NEW DIRECTIONS FOR EVALUATION SERIES
*Jennifer C. Greene, Gary T. Henry,* Editors-in-Chief